A POLITICAL ORGANIZATION APPROACH TO TRANSNATIONAL TERRORISM

Recent Titles in
Contributions in Political Science
Series Editor: Bernard K. Johnpoll

A Political Organization Approach to Transnational Terrorism

KENT LAYNE OOTS

CONTRIBUTIONS IN POLITICAL SCIENCE,
NUMBER 141

Greenwood Press
NEW YORK
WESTPORT, CONNECTICUT
LONDON

Library of Congress Cataloging-in-Publication Data

Oots, Kent Layne.
  A political organization approach to
transnational terrorism.

  (Contributions in political science, ISSN 0147-1066 ;
no. 141)
  Bibliography: p.
  Includes index.
  1. Terrorism.   2. Coalition (Social sciences)
I. Title.   II. Series.
HV6431.065   1986   303.6′25   85-17030
ISBN 0-313-25105-3 (lib. bdg. : alk. paper)

Library of Congress Catalog Card Number: 85-17030
ISBN: 0-313-25105-3
ISSN: 0147-1066

First published in 1986

Greenwood Press, Inc.
88 Post Road West
Westport, Connecticut 06881

Printed in the United States of America

The paper used in this book complies with the
Permanent Paper Standard issued by the National
Information Standards Organization (Z39.48-1984).

10 9 8 7 6 5 4 3 2 1

To the memory of David L. Peterson and Harold D. Oots

CONTENTS

TABLES

ABBREVIATIONS

ACLU	American Civil Liberties Union
AF	Al-Fatah
ANOVA	analysis of variance
BRRF	Bandera Roja, Red Flag
BSO	Black September Organization
CALAI	Comite Argentino de Lucha Anti-Imperialisto
CIA	Central Intelligence Agency
CMB	Commando Muhammed Boudia
CYG	Cuban Youth Group
EC	El Condor
ERP	Ejercito Revolucionario del Pueblo
FALN	Armed Front for National Liberation
ICAO	International Civil Aviation Organization
ICPSR	Inter-University Consortium for Political and Social Research
IRA	Irish Republican Army
ITERATE	International Terrorism: Attributes of Terrorist Events
JRA	Japanese Red Army
L1	LAOS People Number One
L13	LAOS Number Thirteen
NLAF	National Liberation Armed Forces

NSN	nonstate nation
OPEC	Organization of Petroleum Exporting Countries
PFLP	Popular Front for the Liberation of Palestine
PLO	Palestine Liberation Organization
PRC	People's Republic of China
ROC	Republic of China
UAR	United Arab Emirates
UN	United Nations
USSR	Union of Soviet Socialist Republics

ACKNOWLEDGMENTS

Many people have contributed to bringing this project to completion. Thanks are due especially to Tom Wiegele whose extensive comments at every stage were most helpful. Ladd Thomas, Gordon Hilton, and Kurt Wenner also offered helpful and thoughtful comments on earlier versions of the manuscript. Their help has contributed to whatever merit this study has.

Northern Illinois University, and especially the Department of Political Science, provided the support which allowed me to complete this work. I have benefitted as well from discussions with several of my colleagues within the Department of Political Science at NIU. Sung-Soo Joo, Moshe Czudnowski, and Clark Neher have been particularly helpful.

The data used in this study were collected by Edward F. Mickolus and made available in machine-readable format by the Inter-University Consortium for Political and Social Research. Both deserve thanks for making this extensive database available for research.

I also wish to thank James T. Sabin and the editorial staff of Greenwood Press. Their helpfulness and efficiency have made this entire experience less harrowing.

Finally, my wife, Christine, has provided constant encouragement and prodding during the course of my work. She has also patiently suffered through my occasional grumpiness during the course of the project.

While many people have contributed in innumerable ways to this work, final responsibility for the content rests with the author.

A POLITICAL ORGANIZATION APPROACH TO TRANSNATIONAL TERRORISM

I

INTRODUCTION

Terrorism as a phenomenon in the international system over the last decade and a half has spawned a new field of academic study. The field, which for lack of a better term can be referred to as terrorism scholarship, is an eclectic undertaking which includes scholarship from history, economics, sociology, law, and political science. The field has produced works which range from impressionistic essays to empirical and deductive theories, although there are many more of the former than the latter. The field has so far not produced any general theories of terrorist behavior, and many studies still start from an atheoretical orientation. Many works are impressionistic, descriptive, and idiographic. It is not surprising that this is the case in an emerging field of study, since preliminary observation and conceptualization must precede the construction of general theories.

Several problems result from such an approach, however. Impressionistic studies, lacking an empirical basis, can mistake impressions for reality and the preferences of the author can become the theory. Propositions are developed but not tested and are treated as factual without evidence. Such propositions may then find their way into the literature where they are repeated and given the status of knowledge.[1]

Nevertheless, descriptive studies are useful in developing theories. They can provide the preliminary observations which lead to theory development. The difficulty is that descriptive studies are often simply collections of facts which have no apparent connection and no explanatory value.

Idiographic and historical studies may also provide useful observations from which to develop theories of behavior. The problem with such studies, however, is that particular events or cases may be mistaken for the general state of affairs. Simply finding that the behavior of a particular terrorist group is of a specific type does not imply, of course, that all terrorist groups will behave in the same way.

The present study is not a critique of the existing literature. No attempt is made to systematically demonstrate the flaws in previous studies.

The criticisms suggested above are partly the result of the current state of understanding of terrorism as a phenomenon. A great deal of further work must be done before our understanding of the subject is fully developed. This study is constrained, in many ways, by the current level of understanding. The criticisms cited above are meant only to point out the general state of affairs in terrorism studies, not to condemn past efforts. The present study alone will not provide a mature understanding of terrorism. It will, hopefully, be a step in that direction.

What this study will do is examine transnational terrorism and develop an understanding of how two key variables, the presence of coalitions and the size of the acting terrorist group, affect the transnational terrorist act. This will be done by testing hypotheses derived from a theoretical base which treats transnational terrorist groups as nonstate actors in the international system. Specifically, these actors are treated as political organizations, i.e., interest groups. The definition of political organizations will be clarified in a later chapter. For present purposes it is sufficient to say that political organizations are groups whose goals include, but need not be limited to, the provision of public goods.

To accomplish this task the study is divided into several chapters. In this introduction, the limits of the study are established through the development of a usable definition of transnational terrorism. Some of the general literature on terrorism is also reviewed. The role of transnational terrorism is discussed in Chapter 2. Chapter 2 also develops the theory and hypotheses to be tested. A review of previous quantitative studies is presented, along with reviews of public choice studies of terrorism, and previous writings on group size and coalitions. Following these reviews a theory which treats transnational terrorist groups as political organizations and the hypotheses tested are presented.

The data used in testing the hypotheses are also described in Chapter 2. Chapters 3 and 4 present the results of the testing of these hypotheses. Chapter 5 discusses the policy implications of the current study. Finally, Chapter 6 presents the theoretical conclusions derived from the study.

TRANSNATIONAL TERRORISM: A DEFINITION

Terrorism has been defined in various ways by different scholars. Bell (1978b: 97) argues that "[t]errorism is the weapon of the weak, but it is a very powerful weapon." Bell's description treats terrorism as conflictual behavior by those for whom full-scale military conflict is impractical. Fromkin (1978: 19-20) takes a similar approach in arguing that military action is aimed at physical destruction while terrorism aims at psychological consequences. Terrorism, he alleges, is violence for purposes of creating fear. Jenkins (1978a: 239) views terrorism as a new form of warfare. Deutsch (1982) sees terrorism as a low-cost type of warfare between major powers.

The argument that terrorism is a form of warfare is extended by Mallin (1978), who sees terrorism as a military tactic, a type of psychological warfare, used when full-scale military action is not possible. Terrorism, he argues, can be employed as a military weapon under any of three conditions. It may be used as a substitute for normal war, as an addition to normal war, or as the chosen weapon of conflict by one group against another. Terrorism has three functions: psychological consequences, material damage, and economic destruction. As a form of warfare, terrorism is intended to serve political ends (Fromkin, 1978: 119-125).

Paust (1977: 20-21) defines terrorism as "a form of violent strategy, a form of coercion utilized to alter the freedom of choice of others." Paust thus sees terrorism as a tactic which one segment of society can use to constrain the behavior of another. Terrorism, he argues (1977: 21), involves the use or threat of violence against a secondary target in order to communicate a threat to the primary target for purposes of coercing the primary target into granting a particular political outcome.

Paust (1977) has identified one of the key elements of terrorism: It is intended to alter the behavior of the primary target. The immediate target of the terrorists (the victims, a building, etc.) is instrumental. It serves as a symbol to attract attention and gain political concessions from the primary target. The immediate target need not have a clear relation to the primary target.

The Japanese Red Army attack on travellers at Lod Airport in 1972 demonstrates the thrust of Paust's (1977) arguments. The people killed in the attack simply happened to be present at the time and had no clear connection to the primary target of the attack. The immediate victims were tourists; the real target was Israel.[2]

The relation of the immediate target to the primary target is dicussed by Rapoport (1977: 49), who asserts that "[a] terrorist crime is a crime for publicity." Terrorists do not observe the normal restraints of conventional or guerrilla warfare. Terrorists may strike at targets which are related to the primary target only marginally, if at all (Rapoport, 1977: 47-49).

Carlton (1979: 201) defines terrorism as substate violence of a political nature. Jenkins (1982c: 11-12) points out that the word *terrorism* is often used loosely to cover a variety of violent acts. He argues that terrorism is crime, but crime with a political purpose. Terrorism is intended to produce publicity for a political end. Unlike ordinary criminals, terrorists desire to take credit for their actions. Moreover, he argues, terrorism is intended to have consequences beyond the immediate damage inflicted. Thus, again it is argued that the primary target of terrorism is not usually the immediate target; terrorism is instrumental violence.

Jenkins (1978a: 235) makes clear the instrumental character of terrorism, arguing that even though it is often described as senseless violence, terrorism is a means to an end. Turk (1982: 121-122) outlines the components of terrorism. First, terrorism is purposive violence, a means to an end. Second, it has objectives which may be instrumental or expressive. Third, it is targeted violence, with the target being chosen for tactical reasons. Fourth, it is organized violence.

Devine and Rafalko see terrorism as a violent political strategy directed against innocent people. It is characterized by the fact that terrorists claim responsibility for their acts and by victims who are symbolically associated with the real target (Devine and Rafalko, 1982: 40). The definition presented by Devine and Rafalko is narrow. It depends on an ability to determine who is innocent and neglects the possibility of attacks against entities other than people.

Hamilton (1978b: 23) defines terrorism as violence with four distinguishing characteristics. It is planned, has a political purpose, is directed against the state or other established power, and is conducted by a small group.

Kirk (1983: 41-43) describes terrorism as "political extortion." Terrorism may be criminal, i.e., motivated by profit, or it may be ideological, i.e., for purposes of influencing a government. Terrorists, in his view, are utility (profit) maximizers who, through terrorist acts, seek to gain at the expense of the government.

In this section a variety of descriptions of terrorism have been offered. Definitions of terrorism include the following:

1. Terrorism may be a psychological or military act designed to create fear, or cause material or economic destruction.
2. Terrorism may be a method of constraining the behavior of others. This is often done through attacks on victims other than the real target of the act.
3. Terrorism has been described as a crime committed for publicity.
4. Terrorism may be a crime with a political purpose.
5. Terrorism has been described as purposive violence.

6. Terrorism may be a criminal act committed for political or economic gain.

A preliminary definition of terrorism can be offered at this
point which will serve as the basis for further delineation of
the subject of this study. Terrorists in this study are regarded
as rational actors in the sense that they are expected to act in
a manner which they believe will maximize their utility, i.e.,
maximize the gains they make from terrorist acts. Terrorism
in general is an act of violence or a threat of violence committed in order to gain concessions from a primary target as distinguished from an immediate target. Before transnational
terrorism is distinguished from other types of terrorism, it will
be useful to review some other typologies of terrorism.

Typologies of Terrorism

Several scholars have attempted to distinguish between
various types of terrorism. Kirk (1983: 42) distinguishes between criminal terrorism, which is for economic profit, and
ideological terrorism, which is intended to influence government behavior. Merari (1978: 332) differentiates homofighters, who commit terrorist acts against the government or other
domestic groups, from xenofighters, who act against foreign
targets.

Holton (1978: 266) groups terrorism into three classes. Type
I terrorism is committed by small groups or individuals. Type
II terrorism is conducted by governments. When governments
give support to or hire type I terrorists, type III terrorism results. It is a mixture of types I and II.

Attacks in the United States by the Armed Front for National Liberation (FALN) constitute a case of type I terrorism,
while the Nazi genocide during World War II is clearly type
II terrorism. Libya's financial backing of certain terrorist groups
is type III terrorism (Holton, 1978: 266-270).[3]

Shultz and Sloan (1980a: 4) contrast five types of terrorist
groups: ethnic separatists, nationalists, ideological extremists, issue-based interest groups, and sociopathic groups or
individuals. A group can fall within more than one category.

Wilkinson (1979b: 104) divides terrorist organizations into four classes. The first class contains nationalist, autonomous, or ethnic minority groups. The second class consists of ideological sects or secret societies seeking to attain some concept of "revolutionary justice." The third class consists of exile or émigré groups. The fourth class contains transnational groups whose goal is "world revolution." He argues that nationalist groups are the most likely to succeed because there is a natural resentment on the part of the population against foreign rule.

Shultz (1978: 8-10) sees terrorism as goal-directed behavior for political purposes and divides terrorists into three classes. Revolutionary terrorists seek complete social change, sub-revolutionary terrorists seek "structural-functional" changes in the political system, and establishment terrorists wish to prevent changes and preserve the current authority.

Several different types of terrorism have been delineated in this section. The variety of types is demonstrated by the list below.

1. Ideological terrorism is committed in order to influence government.
2. Criminal terrorism is committed for economic gain.
3. Type I terrorism is committed by autonomous groups.
4. Type II terrorism is committed by governments.
5. Type III terrorism is committed by government-supported groups.
6. Nongovernmental terrorist groups may be further divided into several classes: ethnic, ideological, issue-based, nationalist, and sociopathic.

Terrorism can be divided into a number of categories based on tactics, objectives, or targets. The concern of this study is transnational terrorism. A usable definition of transnational terrorism must, therefore, be developed.

Transnational Terrorism

Shultz and Sloan (1980a: 2) are among those who differentiate between transnational terrorism and other types of terrorism. Domestic terrorism, they contend, is carried on within a single state. State terrorism is conducted by a government against its own population. International terrorism is controlled by the state, but occurs outside its borders. Transnational terrorism occurs in the international system and is not state-controlled.

Fearey (1978: 25) defines international terrorism as a politically motivated criminal act which transcends national boundaries. Milbank (1978: 54) describes terrorism as violence intended to influence a target audience, not necessarily the immediate victims, and distinguishes between international terrorism, which is state-controlled, and transnational terrorism, which is conducted by basically autonomous non-state actors.

Pierre (1976: 1252) defines international terrorism as "acts of violence across national boundaries, or with clear international repercussions. . . . " International terrorism, according to Pierre, is conducted by nongovernmental actors, although they may receive governmental support.

Farrell (1982: 12) asserts that "[t]errorism is a purposeful human activity primarily directed toward the creation of a general climate of fear designed to influence, in ways desired by the protagonist, other human beings and, through them, some course of events." International terrorism, he argues, is state-controlled while transnational terrorism is conducted by autonomous groups or individuals.

Transnational terrorism is an act, according to Farrell, which occurs outside the state of which the perpetrator is a citizen. It is conducted either outside the target state or within the target state against a national of another state, or against a target of a different nationality than the offender. It is intended to damage the interests of a state or an international organization. Finally, the act is not committed by or against members of the armed forces during military hostilities (Farrell, 1982: 12-13).

Jenkins (1978a: 238-239) defines international terrorism simply as terrorist acts with international consequences. Terrorist acts are acts of violence outside the accepted norms of diplomacy and war. In a later work (Jenkins, 1982c: 13), he argues that government terrorism is generally internal while international terrorism usually is conducted by nongovernmental groups.

The definition used in this study is that developed by Mickolus (1977c, 1978d, 1979b, 1981, 1983). Transnational terrorism involves the use or threat of "anxiety-inducing extranormal violence" for political purposes by groups or individuals. The act may be conducted in favor of or against an established government. It is not, however, conducted by a government nor is it state-controlled. It is intended to influence an audience wider than the immediate victims. Moreover, because of the nationalities of the perpetrators, the nature of the victims, foreign ties of the perpetrators, location of the act, or the "mechanics of resolution," it transcends national boundaries.

Four types of terrorism are distinguished by Mickolus (1978d: 45; 1979b: 149). Internal terrorism by the government is state terrorism. Internal nongovernmental terrorism is domestic terrorism. Terrorism which transcends national boundaries is either transnational or international. International terrorism is state-controlled. Transnational terrorism is conducted by autonomous groups or persons who may or may not receive some type of government assistance.[4] This study will use the definition offered by Mickolus and delineated above.

Mickolus (1977c: 210-211) lists examples of each kind of terrorism.

1. State terrorism includes the Nazi holocaust and torture of citizens by police states.
2. Domestic terrorism includes attacks on fellow Irishmen by the Irish Republican Army and the Ulster Defense Association.
3. Transnational terrorism includes, for example, many attacks on foreign diplomats and the hijacking of planes.
4. Interstate terrorism includes the anti-Basque campaign in France waged by Spanish authorities.

A clarification is necessary at this point. In this study the term transnational terrorism is used to refer only to terrorism which is not state-controlled. If it is necessary to refer to state-controlled terrorism, it is referred to as interstate, although the primary concern of this study is with transnational terrorism.[5]

A usable definition of transnational terrorism has now been offered. The definition does not take into account the arguments of those who, for ideological reasons, prefer the designations "revolutionary" or "freedom fighter" to "terrorist." These preferences may be important in an ideological sense, but this study is not concerned with ideological definitions of terrorism. It is possible to develop a workable definition of a phenomenon for purposes of study without engaging in an ideological debate as to whether it should be designated by one term or another.

PREVIOUS STUDIES OF TERRORISM

A large body of literature has developed around the subject of terrorism. A number of works, for example, have dealt with the social and political aspects of terrorism (Watson, 1976; Karber and Mengel, 1983; Targ, 1979; Knauss and Strickland, 1979; Thompson, 1976; Lasswell, 1978; Quainton, 1983; Pierre, 1978; Smart, 1978). Hubbard (1983) focuses on the psychological aspects of terrorist behavior. McClure (1978) discusses the possible future of terrorism. Bell (1978a) and Hyams (1975) treat the subject in a general way. Horowitz (1983) discusses the consequences resulting from terrorism becoming a routine event. Jenkins (1982c) focuses on the problems of trying to communicate with terrorists.

Other studies have been more specific. Wilkinson (1979a) reviews theories of terrorist aggression. Ferracuti (1982: 138-139) reviews, and rejects as inadequate, four theories of terrorism. He reviews the "Olson Theory" (rational choice), psychological theory (frustration-aggression), the imbalance of the social system theory, and the Marxist theory.

Another study outlines the supposed dilemmas faced by the terrorists. The first dilemma affects terrorists who are loyal to the cause, but not violent. The dilemma is how to terrorize without causing death or injury. The second dilemma concerns the risk-reward trade-off faced by the terrorists. Should they seek the personal safety of a hit-and-run action or the potential publicity of a protracted, negotiated event? The third dilemma concerns choosing the proper level of violence. An act without sufficient violence may be ignored by the public and the press. An overly violent act may bring a quick show of force from the government and eliminate any possibility of negotiation. In either case the political message of the event becomes lost. The fourth dilemma faces the individual terrorist who may lose his objectivity when a "group think" process sets in among the group. The final dilemma for the terrorists is the necessity of moral legitimacy. How can terrorists create an image which presents them as a powerful force and as victims at the same time (Knutson, 1980: 199-216)?

Bonanate (1979: 57-60) develops a typology of models of terrorism. The South American model, prevalent throughout Latin America, uses kidnapping as its basic tactic. The Middle Eastern model, used by the Palestinian resistance, is aimed at a particular state, Israel, but uses tactics, such as hijacking, which draw other nations into the conflict. The interstate terrorism model consists of terrorism by state actors. Finally, the "pure-international" terrorism model concerns the "balance of terror" among the superpowers, the United States and the Soviet Union.

Cooper (1978a) focuses on the problems terrorism presents for the intelligence community. O'Ballance (1978) discusses terrorism as a form of warfare. Friedlander (1977) studies the historical and legal background of transnational terrorism. Cooper (1978b: 275) looks at terrorism by states and argues that it is increasing.

Another study argues that terrorism is basically an urban phenomenon. Urban settings are ideal for terrorist recruitment because they contain many dissatisfied individuals, and because the contrast of wealth and poverty is more salient in urban areas. Moreover, terrorist groups and individuals can cause more damage in an urban area than in a rural setting (Grabosky, 1979: 51-54).[6]

Bell (1975) divides terrorism into several classes: psychotic, criminal, endemic, authorized (state-directed), vigilante, and revolutionary. Hacker (1976: 8-10) divides terrorists into crusaders, criminals, and crazies. Crusaders generally are organized into pseudo-military units; criminals are organized in a businesslike manner; crazies are usually loners.

Many myths have been perpetuated about terrorism in recent years. Laqueur (1978: 287-290) lists seven of those myths.

1. Terrorism is a new tactic.
2. Terrorism is a left-wing tactic.
3. Terrorism results from legitimate grievances which could be corrected with a resulting end to terrorism.
4. Terrorism is an effective tactic.
5. More destructive weapons will make terrorism a more important tactic.
6. Terrorists are less cruel and more intelligent than other criminals.
7. Terrorists are poor, hungry, desperate individuals.

Stohl (1979a: 2) lists seven additional myths about terrorism.

1. Terrorism is always directed against governments.
2. Terrorism is meant to cause chaos.
3. Terrorism is conducted by crazy people.
4. Insurgency and terrorism are identical.
5. Governments always oppose nongovernmental terrorism.
6. Terrorism is always the result of the internal political situation.
7. Terrorism is a futile strategy.

While Laqueur labels the belief that terrorism is effective as a myth, Stohl labels as a myth the belief that it is a futile strategy. In all likelihood it is neither always futile nor always effective. The fact that such contradictory beliefs exist, however, points to the need for more and better empirical work on terrorism.

A few scholars have sought to develop a profile of the "typical terrorist." He is described as a male, early twenties, single, urban, upper- or middle-class, and educated, usually having some university training. He is also described as a moral absolutist, uncompromising, and risk neutral—his devotion to the cause is more important than consideration of personal risks (Jenkins, 1982b: 15).

Russell and Miller (1978: 82-89) also profile the normal terrorist as urban, single, upper- or middle-class, and educated to the university level. Most terrorists are 22 to 25 years old. However, captured members of the Popular Front for the Liberation of Palestine (PFLP) and Black September Organization (BSO) are usually in their late twenties. Captured Japanese Red Army (JRA) members average 28 years of age. Members of the Baader-Meinhof group in West Germany average 31.3 years of age. The leadership of most organizations is somewhat older than are the operatives.

Amos and Stolfi (1982) and Kupperman, Opstal, and Williamson (1982) are among those who focus on policy and tactical responses to terrorism. Monroe (1982) chronicles the role of the Federal Bureau of Investigation in combatting terrorism in the United States. Mickolus (1978c) discusses arguments for and against negotiating with terrorists holding hostages. Horowitz (1977) considers the possible effects of antiterrorism measures on civil liberties in democratic societies.

Motives, Causes, and Purposes

Several studies, such as those by Lumbsden (1983) and Zawodny (1978), focus on the motives, causes, and purposes of terrorism. Pierre (1976: 1254-1256) lists several motives for terrorism: attainment of political goals; publicity for the cause; undermining of established authority; expression of frustration when no legitimate redress of grievances is possible; obtaining freedom for jailed colleagues; and obtaining money to finance further operations. Rapoport (1977: 48) argues that terrorism serves as a form of therapy for the terrorists as well as a means of evoking a reaction from society.

Another study discusses several possible purposes of terrorism. It can be used to gain specific concessions from the authorities; to gain publicity; to create disorder, collapse the social system, and provoke repression with the ultimate goal of collapsing the government; to punish enemies, for whom the immediate victims are symbols; and to enforce obedience, a goal of state-directed terrorism (Jenkins, 1978a: 236-238).

Terrorism may be used by states as a low-cost form of warfare. States may also support nongovernmental terrorists for use as surrogate soldiers and thus be able to maintain a plausible denial (Jenkins, 1978a: 243-244).

Scalapino (1983: 175) argues that the goal of terrorism is to bring about changes in the leadership, structure, or policies of a particular state. Clutterbuck (1975: 27) argues that the postulated goal of terrorism is the betterment of the lower class. Given the middle- and upper-class backgrounds of the terrorists themselves, he alleges, this claim is not plausible.

Friedlander (1983: 49) argues that the goal of terrorism is a mixture of political goals and financial gain. Wardlaw (1982: 35-39) asserts that the goals of terrorism include instilling fear through unpredictable violence, publicity, and specific social and political concessions.

Devine and Rafalko (1982: 45-50) discuss the arguments mitigating for and against terrorism as a tactic. In favor of terrorism it can be argued that it is the cheapest way to wage war against established authorities. It can also raise the consciousness of the people against the government. The collective guilt argument, that the victims are not really innocent since they did not oppose the alleged repression which the terrorists seek to end, also favors terrorism. Against terrorism it can be argued that it can be counterproductive since it may strengthen the resolve of the authorities not to accede. It may also be ineffective because its demands could not reasonably be met, or because it is often aimed at regimes where other means of political participation are available. For example, terrorism requires publicity which can only come with a free press and other means of communication.

Crenshaw (1981: 383) argues that terrorism has two root causes: the existence of real grievances and the lack of other opportunities for political participation. This argument is contrary to Devine and Rafalko's (1982) claim that terrorism is aimed at regimes that do allow other forms of participation.

Again, such contradictions point to the need for more and better empirical work and less impressionistic work.

Crenshaw (1981) outlines possible motives for terrorism and also for individual participation in terrorism. Terrorism may be motivated by the desire to disrupt the government. It may also be a rational choice strategy, i.e., a useful means of opposing an existing government. It may also be motivated by a desire to affect public attitudes. Terrorism can be motivated by the desire to evoke a repressive response, thereby demonstrating the truth of the terrorist's argument that the government is repressive. It can be motivated by a lack of patience with other methods of obtaining change. It can also be used to serve the internal needs of the terrorist organization, e.g., discipline and morale (Crenshaw, 1981: 385-388).

Individual participation in terrorism may also be motivated by any of several factors. Individual terrorists must possess a willingness to take risks, and to live and act under stress. Solidary benefits may induce an individual to participate in terrorism. Vengeance on behalf of associates may be another reason why individuals participate in terrorism. Shared guilt and the need for moral justification may raise the level of solidarity in the group. Personal feelings of guilt may also induce an individual to become a terrorist (Crenshaw, 1981: 393-395).

The formulation presented by Crenshaw (1981) views terrorists as risk neutral actors. They must view the cause of the group as more important than personal risk, even though this view may result from guilt feelings.

Many motives for terrorism have been postulated in the literature. In this study an assumption is made that terrorists are motivated by the desire for two types of goods, either singly or in combination. First, terrorists may be motivated by the desire to obtain public goods. Public goods include such goods as regime change, freedom for political prisoners, and a Palestinian state as well as such everyday goods as roads, bridges, schools, and national defense. The definition of public goods will be discussed in Chapter 2. For now it is sufficient to say that public goods are goods which are provided by the government and are available to all members of a particular class whether they contribute to the supply of the goods or not;

i.e., it does not matter whether they are terrorists or by-
standers. Such goods may be beneficial (have positive utility)
to some segments of society and be harmful (have negative
utility) to others. A new regime, for example, may have some
impact on all members of society. It will have a positive impact on some, a negative impact on others, and still others may
be indifferent to the change. The major point here is that actors' positive or negative utility is unrelated to their participation in the supply of the good.

Terrorists may also be motivated by a second type of good,
selective incentives. Selective incentives may be either economic or solidary. Selective incentives are goods which are
available only to members of the organized group which seeks
a public good, i.e., the terrorist organization members. Group
solidarity and financial gains from terrorist acts are examples
of selective incentives for terrorists. Selective incentives, along
with coercion in some organizations such as labor unions, are
used by leaders to induce potential members to join an organization which seeks a public good. A desire for the public good
alone is usually not sufficient to induce participation.[7] Moe
(1980) assumes, as does this study, that individuals may be
induced to participate in an organization, in this case a terrorist organization, if they believe that the sum of the utility
of their contributions is less than the sum of the utility of the
benefits offered by the group (solidary, economic, and public
goods). This assumption allows such goods as the desire to take
risks and adventure to be viewed as selective incentives for
the potential terrorist. Selective incentives are a secondary
consideration in this work, however, because the focus is on
the transnational terrorist act. The fact that an act has been
committed presupposes an existing organization and implicitly assumes that the actors in the group have been offered
sufficient inducements to participate. It is assumed that they
view the benefits of participation as being greater than the
costs. The formative stage of the organization is not considered.

In this study an assumption is made that transnational terrorists are motivated by a rational behavior system which leads
them to seek the greatest possible utility under the given con-

ditions. This section, however, has also presented several other possible motivations for terrorist activity which previous scholars have posited. Among those motives are:

1. Terrorism may be committed for publicity.
2. Terrorism may be committed in order to undermine authority.
3. Terrorism may be the result of a need to express frustration.
4. Terrorism may be committed in order to free jailed colleagues.
5. Terrorism may be motivated by a need for financial resources to fund future terrorist operations.
6. Terrorism may be a therapeutic act for the terrorist.
7. Terrorism may be motivated by a desire to provoke repression.
8. Punishment of enemies is another reason for terrorism.
9. Terrorism may be used as a substitute for full-scale warfare.
10. Financial gain may motivate terrorism.
11. Terrorism may be used to create disorder in society.
12. Terrorism may result from a lack of other means for addressing grievances.
13. Terrorism may be a rational choice activity under the given conditions.
14. Collective or personal guilt can motivate the terrorist.
15. Terrorism may be used to demonstrate the group's ability to act.
16. Terrorism may be used to recruit new members for the group.

Thus, a number of motives have been postulated for terrorism. This study assumes that terrorists are making a rational choice decision when they participate in acts of terrorism. Their goals or motives may take any of several forms; however, they view terrorism as the best way to attain their goals under the circumstances. That is, they seek to maximize utility, which results from the attainment of any goal, insofar as it is possible under the given conditions.

Tactics and Targets of Terrorism

Several studies have focused on the methods used by terrorist groups in attempting to achieve their goals. Russell (1983:

55) argues that businesses are the favorite target of terrorists. Another study argues that the modern environment, i.e., the technologically dependent world, gives terrorists a wide array of targets. Communication and transportation systems can be disrupted with large-scale consequences. Moreover, the modern environment gives the anonymous terrorist great freedom of movement (Stiles, 1978: 263-265).

Jenkins (1982b: 13-14) points out that terrorists have not generally committed acts with massive casualties and that six tactics, i.e., bombing, kidnapping, assassination, armed assault, hijacking, and barricade and hostage episodes, account for 95 percent of all terrorist acts. He also argues that terrorist organizations generally use only a limited number of tactics and no organization uses all six of the major tactics. If Jenkins is correct, there is little creativity in terrorist tactics. Tactics are generally imitated, and each organization is limited to the use of a few tactics.

Merari (1978: Table 1, p. 333) classifies groups into four types according to whether their target is foreign or domestic and whether their base of operations is foreign or domestic. Xenofighters, who attack foreign targets, use less discriminate tactics than do homofighters, whose targets are domestic. Either type of group can be foreign or domestically based. Foreign-based groups are likely to commit international terrorism and usually depend upon the support of foreign countries (Merari, 1978: 340-342).

Examples of the four types of terrorist groups are given by Merari (1978: 333).

1. Domestically based xenofighters. These groups have a domestic base and foreign target. The Mau-Mau is an example of this type of group, being based in Kenya, but aimed at the British.

2. Domestically based homofighters. A domestic base and a domestic target mark this category of terrorist groups. The Ejercito Revolucionario del Pueblo, an Argentine group which attacks other Argentines, is an example of a domestically based homofighter group.

3. Foreign-based xenofighters. This class of terrorist groups attacks foreign targets and is based outside its homeland. The immediate target and the primary target of their attacks may be different

entities. The Free Moluccan Youth Movement provides an example of a foreign-based xenofighting group. They are based in Holland, often attack Dutch citizens, but have as their primary target Indonesia.

4. Foreign-based homofighters. This type of group attacks its own countrymen, but operates from a base outside its homeland. The Croatian Revolutionary Brotherhood, whose target is Yugoslavia and whose base is Australia, are foreign-based homofighters.

Another study focuses on the types of weapons available to terrorists. Explosives are easily obtainable and allow simple hit-and-run acts. Automatic weapons may also be used by terrorists. Precision-guided munitions and light anti-tank weapons are available and offer high accuracy and portability. Nuclear weapons are potentially available to terrorists, who would only have to construct a crude, inaccurate weapon to be effective. Finally, chemical and biological weapons could be employed to produce massive destruction (Kupperman, 1979: 5-10).

Carlton (1979: 204) points out that the current world arms trade may allow terrorists to obtain increasingly sophisticated weapons. Nonetheless, he argues (1979: 209), many groups do not desire to cause massive destruction since the leadership of the groups is rational and has developed specific goals.

Jenkins (1979: 4-6) argues that little is known about how terrorist organizations make decisions and the behavioral pattern of terrorists. He lists several factors which could affect the tactics used by a terrorist group.

1. Background of the membership, e.g., previous military training.

2. Size of the acting group.

3. Cultural background.

4. Ideology.

5. Idiosyncracies of key actors.

6. Circumstances of the act, e.g., geographic location.

7. Universal "rules of the game."

The previous studies suggest that many factors, some of which have yet to be investigated, may affect the operations of terrorist groups. They also suggest that terrorism is imitative. There is very little originality, and in spite of the availability of weapons, mass destruction is not generally a tactic of terrorism.

Whatever tactics may be chosen, terrorism is not necessarily a futile strategy. Fearey (1978: 27) reports on Rand Corporation calculations on the effectiveness of terrorism. A terrorist kidnapper can expect to escape death or capture in 89 percent of all cases. Moreover, the terrorist has about an even chance of obtaining all or part of the demanded ransom. It is not simply a futile act.

Scalapino (1983: 175-176), however, reports on why terrorism is not always effective. To be effective in obtaining their ultimate goals terrorists need an enduring organization and the support of an "external populace." Building an effective organization is difficult for several reasons. First, there is a general lack of ideological fervor among most populations. Second, the issues upon which terrorist organizations are built are becoming fewer. Third, government antiterrorist policies in many areas have been effective in preventing the building of long-term organizations. Finally, organizations do not endure because they fail to obtain their goals. Scalapino (1983: 176) further argues that international terrorism cannot be effective without the support of a government, external populace, or international organization.

Crenshaw (1983c: 26ff.) suggests that the success of terrorism may be affected by several factors. It may depend on the type of government response it evokes, on the structure of the situation, especially the possibility of popular support, and on the way in which the terrorist group is organized.

Studies of terrorist tactics lead to two conclusions. First, most terrorist acts are one of a very small number of types of acts. Secondly, most acts of terrorism are imitative in nature. Moreover, it can be seen that the effectiveness of terrorism as a tactic is in much dispute among scholars.

TRANSNATIONAL TERRORISM AND INTERNATIONAL RELATIONS

Terrorist Organizations as Nonstate Actors

Few studies have focused explicitly on transnational terrorists as nonstate actors in international relations. Most studies have made an implicit assumption that terrorists are significant actors. In this section, some of the major literature on transnational, nonstate actors in international relations is reviewed and an argument which treats transnational terrorists as nonstate actors in international relations is presented. In the following section the effects of transnational terrorism on the international system are discussed.

Mickolus (1979b: 147) argues that transnational terrorists are a new type of transnational actor in the international system. He implicitly rejects the state-centric view of the international system. Wolfers (1959) asserts that states are the central actors in the international system, but not the only significant actors. Young (1972: 125) states that most scholars still view the nation-state as the major actor in the international system. He defines a state as an entity having central political institutions and a nation as an integrated community. He points out that the state-centric view has been challenged on several grounds.

Integrationists challenge the state-centric model because modern communications, transportation, and technology have led to a "shrinking world" in which activities can be carried out easily across borders. Integrationists view the nation-state as obsolescent. Transnationalists challenge the state-centric model on the grounds that many organizations exist and operate across state boundaries and are based on some membership criterion other than statehood. Indeed, the loyalties of a single individual may be divided between the nation-state and a variety of interests which transcend the boundaries of the state. Many scholars now take a mixed-actor view of the international system in which a variety of types of actors interact (Young, 1972: 125-136).

Nye and Keohane (1971b: 730) define world politics as po-

litical interactions between significant actors. Significant actors have autonomy and resources, and participate in political
relations across state boundaries. Politics, they argue, is the
use of resources, including threat or punishment, in order to
make other actors behave differently than they would otherwise.

In Nye and Keohane's view an actor in international relations does not have to be a nation-state. Briefly stated, an actor needs autonomy and resources sufficient for its purposes.
They argue (1971b: 724-725) that technology has removed many
barriers that separate nations: e.g., trade and communication
do not end at state borders. Moreover, transnationalism affects nation-states by altering their available choices and the
costs of alternative actions.

Definitions of transnationalism are vague. Huntington (1973:
336) states, "An organization is transnational . . . if it carries
on significant centrally-directed operations in the territory of
two or more nation-states." Keohane and Nye (1974: 41) use
the term to refer to nongovernmental actors only. This study
follows their usage. Transnational refers only to nongovernmental actors. This term is further defined below.

Mansbach, Ferguson, and Lampert (1976: 3-4) take a position similar to Nye and Keohane's (1971b) in arguing that an
actor in the international system must possess autonomy; it
need not possess sovereignty or territory. In this study an implicit assumption is made that actors in the international system must have autonomy, but need not have sovereignty, territory, or other characteristics of statehood. Mansbach,
Ferguson, and Lampert (1976: 22-27) even argue that sovereignty is a meaningless term. Nation-states are subject to both
internal and external constraints on their behavior. Indeed,
many states held to be sovereign by international law are not
independent actors, and are sovereign only in a technical sense.
Moreover, some nonstate actors, such as the Palestine Liberation Organization (PLO), possess greater military capabilities, and hence the ability to preserve autonomy, than do many
states.

Using autonomy, rather than sovereignty, as the criterion
for defining actors in the international system leads to a broader

view of what constitutes world politics. Nye and Keohane (1971a: 341) point out that autonomous actors can include trade unions, multinational businesses, revolutionary movements and the Roman Catholic Church, among others.[8] Mansbach, Ferguson, and Lampert (1976: 39-40) list six types of international actors: international governmental organizations (IGOs), international nongovernmental organizations (INGOs), nation-states, noncentral governmental actors, international nongovernmental actors, e.g., labor unions and individual actors. Field (1971) and Skjelsbaek (1971) have focused on the growing number of nongovernmental organizations in the international system.

Nye and Keohane (1971a) discuss the effects of transnationalism in international relations. These include attitude changes, the growth of international pluralism, constraints on state behavior, increased ability of some states to influence others, and the emergence of autonomous actors with private foreign policies.

If transnational terrorism is to be studied as a subfield of international relations, it must be shown that transnational terrorists are significant actors in the international system. Transnational terrorists are not state-controlled and thus have autonomy, although many factors may constrain their behavior as they do the behavior of states. Transnational terrorists may receive some support from governments. They may be influenced by governments or by other groups. This does not diminish their status as actors any more than foreign aid from one government makes another government less of a state. Being subject to constraints and influences does not diminish their status as actors, since these constraints are no more, and may be less, than those affecting nation-states.

Transnational terrorists possess autonomy. It remains to be shown that they are truly transnational. They are transnational in the sense that they are nongovernmental. They are also transnational in the sense that, by the definition presented in the first chapter, their actions affect segments of two or more nations.

It is, for the above reasons, plausible to assume that transnational terrorists constitute a type of autonomous transnational actor. Some transnational terrorist groups may even have the status of a nonstate nation (NSN). Bertelsen (1977a: 2) defines an NSN as "any entity which operates in a manner normally associated with a nation-state but is not generally recognized as a nation-state." The PLO and some ethnic separatist groups by this definition constitute NSNs.[9] Some NSNs direct violence against foreign states in order to avoid being dismissed as simply an internal problem (Bertelsen, 1977b: 251). Terrorist organizations may adopt this same tactic.

Having established that transnational terrorists are autonomous actors in the international system, it is necessary to demonstrate that they are significant actors in the international system. Their significance depends on the extent to which they affect other actors.

The Effects of Transnational Terrorism

Several studies have focused on the significance of transnational terrorism. Crenshaw (1983b) deals with the consequences of transnational terrorism, while Horowitz (1973) gives an impressionistic view of the political consequences of state efforts to stop terrorism. Duggard (1974) discusses the problems faced by international organizations in attempting to define terrorism.

Lord Chalfont (1982: 313) points out that terrorism is a major international phenomenon in three respects. Terrorists do not respect national boundaries, they have significant relations with others outside their own states, and they are often supported by particular states.

Redlick (1979: 75-76) postulates that the transnational flow of communications may be partly responsible for making terrorism a significant phenomenon. Modern communication systems allow those in one state to see the standard of living of those in other states. Feelings of relative deprivation may result which can be a cause of terrorism.[10] Modern communication systems also facilitate contacts among terrorist groups and make it possible for one group to learn vicariously the tactics and justifications of another. Communication systems make terrorism more significant because terrorist acts can be seen and demands heard around the world (Redlick, 1979: 85).

Dror (1983: 90) reasons that terrorism poses a crisis for democratic governments because of their limited ability to respond. Kupperman and Trent (1979: 141) point out that the international community lacks any plan for dealing with terrorism. Responses to terrorism are basically a national responsibility. They also discuss (1979: 112-113) two types of extreme responses and their consequences. A no-concessions policy may have some validity, but would require reconsideration if massive destruction were threatened. Strategic capitulation, at the other extreme, is not viable because success encourages terrorism.

Transnational terrorism, according to Milbank (1978: 55-56), became a major international phenomenon around 1967 when Palestinian guerrilla activity intensified. Beer (1981: 260) contends that the terrorist crisis may become more significant because of the ability of terrorists to threaten the current nuclear balance. Technology, especially in weapons, communications, and transportation has served to make terrorism a more prevalent phenomenon (Wardlaw, 1982: 25). The media, through the use of modern technology, have also served to promote terrorism by providing terrorists with an audience (Milbank, 1978: 60; Wardlaw, 1982: 25). Modern communications also make possible the transnational flow of terrorist ideas (Wardlaw, 1982: 31-32). International interdependence and subnational linkages also encourage terrorism by creating a "crisis of identity," which may lead to terrorism, and also by providing an array of potential targets, e.g., multinational businesses (Milbank, 1978: 60-61).

Milbank (1978: 72) argues that terrorism is likely to increase in the future and that nation-states have only limited abilities to stop it. Carlton (1979: 221-222) argues that states could affect the future of terrorism by cooperating to stop it, leaving things as they are, or actually increasing sponsorship of terrorism. Obviously, only the first option could lead to a reduction in terrorism through state policy. Dror (1983: 69) argues that governments could not stop terrorism because the

causes of terrorism are too numerous to be effectively eliminated. Carlton (1979: 214) argues that two possible methods
for eliminating terrorism, the elimination of the causes of terrorism and ruthless antiterrorist campaigns, are both implau-
sible since they suppose a level of government power which
most states do not possess.

Terrorism has thus been described by the above scholars as
a crisis in the international system. It is viewed by many
scholars as a phenomenon which cannot be eliminated through
the power of the state. Terrorists, from the point of view of
those who wish to end terrorism, are significant actors.

Hutchison (1975, Crenshaw, 1983c) focuses on specific ways
in which transnational terrorists may be significant actors in
the international system. Several of these reasons from
Hutchison (1975: 114-116) are listed below.

1. Terrorism demonstrates that national boundaries can be penetrated without the consent of the state.
2. It demonstrates the ability of small groups to harm the interests
   of governments.
3. Terrorism is a disruptive, rather than stabilizing, force in the international system.
4. It has gained international recognition for its goals.
5. Terrorism demonstrates interdependence in the international system.
6. It undermines the authority of the nation-state.
7. It demonstrates the ineffectiveness of strategic power against low-
   level attacks.
8. Terrorism affects foreign entities in a given area, e.g., foreign corporations operating in a particular nation.
9. It demonstrates the vulnerability of a technologically dependent
   world; e.g., transportation systems can be easily disrupted.

Crenshaw (1983c: 22) asserts that terrorism has a social effect as well. It serves to develop a group identity among participants and polarizes participant views by reinforcing the
image of the opposition as being the enemy.

Terrorism can lead to change in the international system in

at least four ways. First, it can alter the structure of power in the international system. For example, terrorism can lead to the replacement of one regime by another or may be a catalyst for outside intervention in a nation's affairs (Crenshaw, 1983c: 8).

Second, terrorism may lead to an alteration of government policies. Policies may be instituted to curtail terrorism which lead to a lessening of civil liberties. Governments could also attempt to institute policies to eliminate the alleged causes of terrorism, e.g., "political injustice" (Crenshaw, 1983c: 10-13).

Third, terrorism may alter political attitudes. It may promote the polarization of opposing segments of society. It may also be used to curtail participation in the political process by certain segments of society (Crenshaw, 1983c: 14-15).

Fourth, terrorism can alter future patterns of violence in the political system. As a contagious phenomenon it can inspire further violence, and also increase the probability of continued or expanded violence in the political system (Crenshaw, 1983c: 17).

The literature reviewed in this section argues for the conclusion that transnational terrorists are significant actors in the international system. They affect other actors and have the potential, for example by disrupting communications, to affect large segments of the world population. They also can alter and constrain the behavior of nation-states, and thus it is reasonable to describe them as significant actors.

NOTES

1. This situation is not unique to terrorism studies. Lebow (1983: 440-441), for example, traces the often repeated belief that Khrushchev had sized up Kennedy as a weak person during their meeting in Vienna. The idea started as pure speculation, clearly labeled as such, in a column by James Reston of the *New York Times*. It subsequently was repeated many times and became part of the "conventional wisdom" on the Kennedy presidency.

2. In this case the Puerto Ricans who were killed had no relation to the target state, Israel. The JRA apparently was expecting Israeli travellers. The Puerto Ricans simply happened to be in the wrong place at the wrong time. This case demonstrates that victims can

sometimes be chosen randomly and that hardly anyone can be assured of not becoming a victim.

3. Holton's inclusion of the Nazi genocide as terrorism is unusual since the immediate victims and the target were the same and no demands were made of the victims. The victims were not hostages in this case. They were simply marked for execution by the Nazi regime.

4. In later works, however, Mickolus (1981: Figure 2.1, p. 2.8; 1983: 4) alters his typology. What he previously labeled international terrorism he refers to as interstate terrorism, and transnational terrorism becomes international terrorism. The use of the term *interstate terrorism* clarifies the fact that it is state-controlled. International terrorism may be supported by a state but is not state-controlled (Mickolus, 1983: 4).

5. The term *international terrorism* is ambiguous and will not be used by the present author to refer to the subject of this study. Where the term *international terrorism* is used, it is used to refer to the works of other authors who use the term. Often they use the term without careful definition. This difficulty cannot be prevented.

6. Marighella (1971) can be consulted for a fuller discussion of urban terrorism.

7. This discussion generally follows Olson (1971). Olson should be consulted by those desiring a fuller explanation of public goods and selective incentives in organizations.

8. Corsino (1977) demonstrates the relevance of a revolutionary movement as an international actor by tracing the international relations of the Partai Komunis Indonesia.

9. The PLO is among many terrorist groups which do not like to be classified as terrorists. Nonetheless, the PLO did commit several acts during the period covered by the data used in this study which are classifiable as acts of transnational terrorism.

The PLO is an especially difficult group to pin down, however. It is made up of several constituent organizations, most of which do not advocate terrorism.

10. Relative deprivation is not an objective condition. Gurr (1972: 185) defines it as "the actors' perception of the discrepancy between their value expectations . . . and their value capabilities." It is thus the difference between what an actor believes he has a right to expect and what he thinks he can attain under present conditions. The actor's perception is the key factor, since the perceived condition, not the actual condition, is the basis for action.

II

GROUP SIZE AND COALITIONAL ACTIVITIES

QUANTITATIVE STUDIES OF TERRORISM

A sizeable body of literature has been devoted to quantitative studies of terrorism, although the literature is of uneven quality. Most of this work has been descriptive rather than theoretically informed, although there are exceptions. Many studies, for example, have focused on the process of how terrorism spreads from one area to another and whether or not it is an increasing phenomenon, i.e., the so-called "contagion effect" of terrorism (Hamilton and Hamilton, 1983; Midlarsky, Crenshaw, and Yoshida, 1980; Heyman, 1980; Heyman and Mickolus, 1980, 1981). Osmond (1978, 1979) has attempted to explain terrorism using Gurr's (1970) model of civil strife. He concludes (1979: 160), based on a regression model, that the relative deprivation model produces a poor fit for terrorism.

The Central Intelligence Agency (CIA) (1978) uses frequency counts to trace various trends in transnational terrorism over the previous decade. Avery (1981)looks at the role of international arms transfers and terrorism. Wright (1981) performs a time-series analysis of the conflict in Northern Ireland. Winn (1981) uses survey research to study the correlates of support for terrorism among West German university students. Gleason (1981) looks at terrorism in the Third World and concludes (1981: 252) that it is not increasing from year to year.

In another work, Gleason (1980) uses a Poisson model of international terrorist incidents in the United States between January 9, 1968, and April 26, 1974. He concludes (1980: 263-265) that international terrorism did not increase between the first 38 months of the period and the last 38. During the first period the monthly mean was 1.053 incidents. During the second period it was .632. Not only was international terrorism not increasing, overall it was decreasing.

Jenkins (1982a) studies frequencies of attacks by terrorists on diplomats. An earlier study (Jenkins, 1976) focuses on the rate of survival for terrorist hostages. Jenkins and Johnson (1975, 1976) present chronologies of transnational terrorist attacks from 1968 through 1974. Another study (Jenkins, 1978b) reviews trends in international terrorism. Jenkins (1980) speculates on the future of terrorism in the next decade. Jenkins and Ronfeldt (1977) focus again on hostage survival.

Bass and Jenkins (1983: 3-8) review trends in transnational terrorism for 1980 and 1981 using frequency counts. They reach several interesting conclusions. The number of incidents, 250 in 1980 and 326 in 1981, represents an increase of 100 percent over the previous two years. Bombings accounted for 42 percent of the 1980 cases and 51 percent of the 1981 cases. Taken together, bombings, hijackings, barricade and hostage episodes, assassinations, armed assaults and kidnappings accounted for 95 percent of all 1980 and 1981 cases. Moreover, these tactics have changed little over time. Terrorism, as noted previously, is imitative rather than creative. Finally, they found that 90 percent of all terrorist victims are civilians.[1] A similar review of trends in terrorism for 1982 and 1983 is presented by Cordes et al. (1984).

Fowler (1980: 9-10) suggests some preliminary questions to be investigated through quantitative analysis.

1. Are certain patterns of behavior related to a specific group or region?

2. Are certain acts associated with certain groups?

3. Does the "severity" of the act relate to the specific group or to its regional identity?

4. Is terrorist activity related to the attributes of the group (especially size)?

Fowler's questions are very general and are not really testable in their present form. They are, however, related to the understanding of the phenomenon of terrorism and go beyond descriptive studies. There is, however, no overriding theory which links Fowler's (1980) propositions together.

Snitch (1982: 62-64) attempts to correlate socioeconomic variables with frequency of political assassinations. Most of his findings are modest. His strongest results are found when frequency of assassination is correlated with the rate of inflation (.27), percent of labor force in agriculture (−.19), literacy rate (.17), percent of population in urban areas (.22), rate of urban growth (−.16), and life expectancy (.17). Snitch concludes that while the results are not exceptional they point to a higher frequency of political assassination in developed countries rather than the Third World. This is contrary to what Snitch expected to find and leads him to conclude that further efforts are needed to develop explanations for political assassinations.

Hamilton (1978a, 1978b, 1981) attempts to develop a causal theory of terrorism. His doctoral dissertation (1978b) is the most complete presentation of his work. In that work he develops a multivariate causal model of terrorism and tests the model using the civil strife data set collected by Gurr (Hamilton, 1978b: 92-95). The model is applied to three nations: Israel, Canada, and Argentina. Hamilton lays out several conclusions from his work, including:

1. Terrorism is most likely to occur in democratic political systems (1978b; 174).

2. Terrorism provokes punitive repression (1978b: 177).

3. If the terrorists survive the oppression, further terrorism results from the oppression (1978b: 180-181).

4. Terrorism has no effect on the probability of a successful revolution (1978b: 181).

Shultz and Sloan (1980a: 15) use frequency counts and reach the conclusion that there has recently been a large increase in the frequency of international terrorist acts. Gurr (1979: 25) also uses frequency counts and reaches three general conclusions.

1. Terrorism is destructive violence carried out by clandestine, rather than open, means.
2. The principal targets of terrorism are political entities.
3. Terrorist groups operate in sporadic fashion.

Gurr (1979) also studied terrorism for the period from 1961 through 1970 and reached several conclusions about the period.

1. Clandestine groups constitute 69 percent of all terrorist groups while conventional political groups constitute 23 percent (Table 4, p. 34).
2. Property was a target in 67 percent of all cases, public persons in 53 percent, and private persons or groups in 24 percent (Table 7, p. 37).
3. Political purposes could be attributed to 97 percent of all cases (Table 9, p. 39).[2]
4. In 6 percent of all cases the terrorists received foreign support, 12 percent had suspected foreign support, and 27 percent involved foreign targets. Thus, 40 percent of all cases had foreign support or targets (Table 10, p. 41).

Mickolus (1977a, 1977b, 1977c, 1978a, 1978b, 1978c, 1978d, 1979a, 1979b, 1981, 1982, 1983; Mickolus and Heyman, 1981; Mickolus, Heyman, and Schlotter, 1980) has been the most prolific scholar in quantitative terrorist studies. Some of his studies (Mickolus 1978a, 1979a) are simple chronologies of terrorist acts. Other studies (Mickolus, 1978b, 1982; Heyman and Mickolus, 1981) focus on the development of the International Terrorism: Attributes of Terrorist Events database (IT-ERATE). Most of his work has focused on tracking trends in transnational terrorism.

Mickolus and Heyman (1981: Tables 8.1a and 8.1b, p. 157)

look at frequencies of transnational terrorist events between 1968 and 1977. They report that the United States (345 cases) and Argentina (327) are the favorite locations for terrorist acts. The Irish Republican Army (IRA) with 211 events, the Black September Organization (BSO) with 137 cases, and Palestinian terrorists of indeterminate membership with 132 events were the most active groups.

Mickolus (1977c) sketches some trends in international terrorism over time and shows that the type of act committed varies from region to region. Mickolus (1978d: 46-53) lays out several conclusions from his studies.

1. Terrorist groups may also engage in other (legitimate) forms of political activity.
2. Contrary to popular notions, nearly half of all transnational terrorist events between 1968 and 1975 occurred in developed, Western nations.
3. Terrorism has been very successful in gaining publicity.

Mickolus (1981: 3.4-3.5) divides the terrorist event into five phases: planning, initiation, negotiation, climax, and cleanup. He also discusses the ITERATE data base and the sources used to collect the data (1981: 3.10-3.23). He demonstrates (1981: 4.4-4.5) that between 1968 and 1977 there was no linear increase in the frequency of transnational terrorist events.

Mickolus has also briefly treated the size of the terrorist group and links between terrorist groups. These studies are discussed in the fourth section of this chapter.

RATIONAL CHOICE STUDIES OF TERRORISM

A small body of literature has been developed which seeks to understand terrorism as a rational choice process, i.e., a process of choosing among alternative actions in a manner supposed by the actors to be consistent with their utility maximization. Their choices are consistent with their preferred outcomes. When faced with a range of possible actions they will choose the course which they believe offers the best chance of obtaining their preferred outcome.[3]

Fitzgerald (1978) uses a game-theoretic model to explain threats of extortion by terrorists. Leites (1979) argues that terrorist acts are calculated actions carried out in order to obtain the goals of the terrorists, i.e., they are rational acts. These and several other studies view terrorism as a rational choice process. It is treated as a process of rational calculation designed to advance the desires of the terrorists, i.e., to maximize their utility. In these studies terrorists are not viewed as lunatics (as they are in many studies) whose attacks are random and unrelated to any specific goals.

It should again be pointed out that we are not dealing with a psychological classification of "lunatics" here. Rationality does not demand that behavior be in accord with societal norms. Technically, a person can be rational and a lunatic at the same time. For example, a man who spends his time planting bombs in airport lockers can be rational if he really prefers to spend his time that way. Society may nonetheless consider him to be a lunatic since his behavior deviates from that which society classifies as acceptable.

Hilton (n.d.: 1) argues that terrorists are utility maximizing actors. His measure of utility is the abstract concept of political exchange rather than monetary exchange. Hilton's major conclusion (n.d.: 7) is that terrorist threats may result in any of several outcomes. He defines X_0 as the status quo and X_1 as the threatened result of the terrorist act if the terrorists' demands are not met. In order to avoid X_1 the government must pay some risk premium, i.e., give up some amount of political exchange in the form of concessions to the terrorists. The amount given up will lie somewhere between X_0 and X_1. Hilton thus brings the concept of social exchange to the study of terrorism.

Wolf (1978b: 297) views politics as a bargaining process wherein certain values are maximized to the benefit of some groups and the detriment of others. Groups that do not benefit may become angry and seek change, possibly through the use of violence. These groups view violence as simply another bargaining technique.

Osayimwese (1983: 183) sees terrorism as utility maximizing behavior at two levels. It can be used to gain either personal objectives or group objectives. The terrorist has a choice between legal and illegal actions in pursuit of these goals. In making his choice he must consider the expected value of the act of terrorism, the severity of the potential punishment (disutility of the act), and the probability of being caught and punished. He then develops a three-activity model in which, based on individual calculations, the actor may allocate his time among violent crimes, nonviolent crimes, and legal activities. Finally, Osayimwese argues that external costs, e.g., injuries to innocent people, must be considered in calculating the social costs of violence (Osayimwese, 1983: 187-190).[4]

Roeder (1982) attempts to test the theory of "rational revolution" developed by Tullock (1971). Tullock's model can be briefly described here. An actor in a nation beset by a revolution has three choices: join the revolution, join the government's forces, or do nothing. A successful revolution is a public good. The actor will benefit or suffer from the regime change whether he participates in the revolution or not. Moreover, for an individual actor the probability of his actions making a difference one way or another is slight; i.e., the probability that his activity would be a determining factor in the success of the revolution is approximately 0.[5]

It would appear that a rational actor will be better off by not participating on either side. However, the actor will also consider his personal payoff, e.g., the possibility of a government position if the revolution succeeds, in determining whether or not to participate. He must consider the potential payoffs from each side and the risks involved, e.g., death, injury, and punishment. The salient variables in the calculation are risks and rewards. Tullock (1971: 95) concludes that the public good aspect of the revolution does not enter the calculation. No one would take action based on his valuation of the public good because, in Tullock's view, most revolutions consist of one despotic regime replacing another despotic regime. The utility of an individual would not change much in any case. This view is explained by Salert (1976: 24), who states, "[T]he basic contention of the rational-choice explanation is that people participate in revolutionary movements because they derive some personal benefit."

Salert (1976: 24-26) goes on to explain that since revolution is a public good, the chances of an individual actor making a difference are slight. The rational course for an individual is to remain inactive. This results in a free rider problem wherein a person who does not participate in the supply of the public good still benefits from its provision.[6] To overcome the free rider problem, selective incentives must be offered in the form of positive inducements or negative sanctions. Salert (1976: 38) argues that selective incentives may include material rewards, coercion, or psychological gratification. In a few cases, e.g., true leaders of the revolution, individual participation may make a difference and thus the free rider problem does not affect some persons (Salert, 1976: 38).

Kirk (1983: 43) argues that terrorists are profit maximizers. They seek to profit from the terrorist act by gaining concessions from the government. He further argues that the claim that reducing the causes of terrorism by increasing the size of the government will eliminate terrorism is not true. Kirk is assuming an economic rather than an ideological motive for terrorism and argues that increasing the size of the government increases rents (income) to the government. Government rents are what terrorists hope to profit from. Therefore, increasing the size of the government will lead to an increase in terrorism because terrorists will have more to gain.

Sandler, Tschirhart, and Cauley (1983: 38) argue that terrorists are rational actors and thus favor low-risk terrorist acts over high-risk events. They define a rational actor (1983: 38) as "an individual or collective . . . optimizing some goal, usually utility, subject to a set of constraints, restricting the actions that can be taken. These constraints indicate the limits imposed by resources, . . . legal rules, and institutional rules." They thus argue that terrorists are both rational and risk averse.

Sandler, Tschirhart, and Cauley (1983: 39) go on to argue that terrorists may choose between legal and illegal activities in order to maximize utility. They also develop a model of negotiation during terrorist events which includes an element of randomness since neither the terrorists nor the government can be certain what actions the other side will take. Thus, they bring in an element of strategic rationality wherein both the terrorists and the government must attempt to maximize utility subject to a given set of constraints and subject as well to the actions of the other side.

In a later section an attempt is made to fit transnational terrorism into a rational choice theory of political behavior. Propositions about the behavior of terrorists are then derived. In the next section, however, a review of previous work on group size and the presence of coalitions is presented.

STUDIES OF GROUP SIZE AND COALITIONS

Group Size

A few studies have focused on the way in which terrorist groups are organized. Hutchison (1975: 111), for example, argues that even transnational terrorist groups have a local or subnational base. Only a few of these studies of organizations give much attention to the size of the group.

Grabosky (1979: 54-55) states that most terrorist groups are organized in urban areas where the group can be assembled and disbanded quickly. The basic organization is cellular, i.e., the group is divided into many smaller units for security purposes. The normal cell has only three to five members. The acting group, the group actually involved in the terrorist act, is small, averaging only 4.4 members (Mickolus, 1981: 4.22). This is partly because there is an increased security risk among large groups. The more people that know about the plans, members, and resources, the higher the risk (Mickolus, 1981: 5.69).

Wolf (1978a: 170-174) outlines the organization of the urban terrorist group. A group must have goals which form the basis for the organization. The cell is the basic unit of organization for purposes of assigning specific tasks to specific units. Thus, there is a division of labor as different cells perform different duties. A cell generally consists of three to ten members. Cells are then grouped into columns. Each column has specific functions and contains 50 to 300 members. A command council provides the overall direction for the group. The maintenance of this structure requires financial resources, which is why many terrorist acts are committed for monetary gain rather than for the political goals of the group directly.

Further work has shed additional light on the subject of terrorist organizations. One member acts as cell leader and contact person with the higher organizational command. Cell members are given as little information about the organization as is necessary for them to function. They may not even know who the group's members are outside their own cell. Thus, if they are captured they have little information which can be divulged to the authorities. The overall organization normally consists of 1,500 to 2,000 members (Wilkinson, 1979b: 112-113). Gurr (1979: Table 6, p. 35) puts the figure somewhat lower. His figures indicate that 86 percent of the terrorist groups have fewer than 50 members. Another 8 percent have between 50 and 500 and only 6 percent have more than 500.

Very little attention has been paid to the operational consequences of the size of the acting group. Fowler (1980: 10) asks whether group size relates to the type of act committed and whether the size of the overall group affects its activity level. Jenkins (1979) is more specific:

The size of the group may also determine the nature of its activities. It is not simply that a larger group is likely to possess greater resources. The actions of smaller groups may be determined more by the personal idiosyncracies of a single leader. A smaller group may feel more vulnerable to infiltration which may constrain its activities. (P. 5)

Very little attention has been paid in previous studies to the size of the acting terrorist group and its operational consequences. Most of the previous work has focused on describing terrorist organizations and not on how organizational properties, including size, affect the behavior of the terrorist group. This study attempts to further the knowledge of this aspect of terrorist behavior.

Terrorist Coalitions

This study is also concerned with the operational consequences of terrorist coalitions, defined as two or more terrorist groups cooperating to commit an act of terrorism. Few studies have focused on cooperation at the operational level. Several studies have focused generally on links between terrorist groups and between groups and various states (Anable, 1978; Demaris, 1977; Sterling, 1981).

Mickolus (1981: 5.62) points out that joint terrorist operations are rare. He argues (1981: 5.69-5.70) that there are several reasons for this. Since the goals of two groups may differ, cooperation must be negotiated and concessions made. Agreement on operations and goals is difficult to obtain. Personality and ideological differences may also hinder the development of coalitions. Moreover, bringing a second group into an operation increases the number of people who know the resources, plans, and people involved in the act. This presents an increased security risk. Thus, single group, single nationality events are prevalent (Mickolus, 1981: 4.22).

While joint attacks are rare, other types of cooperation between terrorist groups are more common. The PFLP, for example, often gives support to other Middle Eastern groups with similar ideologies (Mickolus, 1981: 5.57). No centrally directed "terrorist international" exists, however (Mickolus, 1981: 5.69). This belief is shared by others (Alexander and Kilmarx, 1979a: 51; Crenshaw, 1983a: 143). Martha Crenshaw Hutchison (1975: 111) states, "Limited operational collaboration among terrorist organizations has taken place, but transnational relations among them are generally not active, formal, institutionalized or overt." Milbank (1978: 58) argues that ad hoc alliances exist between many organizations.

Bell (1975: 72-74) notes that cooperation among groups has occurred. Generally, the groups are ideologically similar and from within the same region. Still other groups may be sponsored by various nation-states.

While still comparatively rare, joint terrorist operations have occurred (Mickolus, 1978d: 57). Several scholars believe that such working relationships are becoming more common. Wardlaw (1982: 55) argues that links and operational cooperation between groups are increasing. Mickolus (1978d: 57; 1983: 17) also believes that links between groups are increasing. Alexander and Kilmarx (1979a: 50-51) state, on the basis of anecdotal evidence, that joint operations are becoming more common.

Aside from joint operations, coordinated (simultaneous) attacks have also occurred. Attacks by proxy, one group attacking a target on behalf of another group, have also taken place. For example, JRA terrorists conducted an attack at Lod Airport in 1972 on behalf of the Palestinian resistance (Alexander and Kilmarx, 1979a: 47-49).

Other forms of cooperation have also taken place. For example, some groups have provided technical and financial help to other groups (Kupperman and Trent, 1979: 22). Mickolus (1978d: 57; 1979b: 164; 1983: 17) argues that the Palestinian resistance has been responsible for training members of various groups from many regions at its training camps in the Middle East. IRA and JRA terrorists as well as others from West Germany and Latin America have been trained at the camps. Mickolus (1978d: 57) also states that some Latin American groups that are successful at obtaining large ransoms have funded other groups with smaller financial resources.

Meetings of terrorists from many nations have also occurred (Mickolus, 1978d: 57). Jenkins (1978a: 242-243) argues that some alliances between specific groups exist, e.g., the alliance between the PFLP and the JRA, and are likely to continue for an extended period of time. In many alliances groups with larger resources provide assistance to other groups. Some ill-equipped groups may thus be able to commit acts which they would be unable to carry out alone. Jenkins (1978a: 243-244) contends that there is the potential for a worldwide terrorist group to develop if cooperation increases. States may also begin to employ terrorist groups as surrogate soldiers, allowing one state to attack another and still maintain a plausible denial.

Modern transportation and communication systems are, in

part, responsible for making terrorist alliances possible. They are also responsible for the possibility of widespread terrorism since any target in the world can be attacked within a matter of hours.

Alexander and Kilmarx (1979a: 40-51) detail several types of cooperation which may occur between groups and between groups and supportive regimes. Among the types of cooperation are

1. *Financial.* For example, the main source of income for Palestinian groups is from certain Arab states. These groups may in turn provide financial support to other groups. Libya is a frequent contributor to terrorism, allegedly giving bonuses to terrorists who attack its enemies. Libya is believed, for example, to have paid a bonus of between $1,000,000 and $2,000,000 to Ilich Ramirez-Sanchez ("Carlos the Jackal") for leading a successful raid on the headquarters of the Organization of Petroleum Exporting Countries (OPEC) in 1975.

2. *Training.* The Middle East is the location of many training camps for terrorists. The camps are run by the PLO and its constituent groups. Camps are also operated by the governments of Algeria, Syria, and Libya. For example, JRA terrorists have trained at PFLP camps since 1970.

3. *Weapons.* Weapons, generally made in communist nations, are supplied by Palestinian terrorists to many other groups. Some Arab states also supply weapons to various groups.

4. *Organizational.* Some groups and supportive governments supply forged documents, propaganda support, and communications support to other groups.

5. *Operational.* Proxy attacks, coordinated attacks, and joint operations, as noted earlier, have also occurred.

Links exist between many governments and transnational terrorist organizations. Mickolus (1979b: 164; 1983: 17) states that Libya, the Soviet Union, the People's Republic of China, some Eastern European regimes, radical Arab states, and North Korea have supported transnational terrorist groups by providing arms, money, and training.

Livingstone (1982: 1) argues that the Soviet Union trains and supports many terrorists as a means of waging low-cost war against the West and obtaining favor among the Third World population. He also argues (1982: 11-17) that other regimes also support terrorism by providing arms, money, and asylum for terrorists. Thus, he believes, transnational terrorism is largely the product of a few states. The Soviet Union is at the helm of this international terrorist movement, although it is moving toward providing support for terrorists through surrogate client states such as Cuba, East Germany, Syria, Libya, and Czechoslovakia.[7] Libya is alleged to support more than 40 groups.

In contrast to other scholars who assert that no "terrorist international" exists, Livingstone (1982) believes that terrorism is basically a single movement directed by the Soviet Union and supported through Soviet client states. Intuitively, his claim appears doubtful given the number of groups that are active and the variety of causes they represent. A good deal of further work would be needed to support such a theory of conspiracy.

Thus far the previous work on group size and coalitions has been reviewed. In the next section a theory is developed from which to derive testable propositions about how these two variables operationally affect transnational terrorism.

TRANSNATIONAL TERRORIST GROUPS AS POLITICAL ORGANIZATIONS

The first issue which must be dealt with in this section is whether or not transnational terrorist groups constitute political organizations in the sense of being political interest groups. Some of the previous literature has constructed the groundwork for such an assertion. Tullock's (1971) theory, for example, treats revolutionary groups as interest groups whose goals consist of public goods. Bell (1971: 505) argues that transnational revolutionary movements should be viewed as transnational political parties. Olson and Zeckhauser (1966: 267-268) treat international organizations, especially alliances, as interest groups, arguing that their major function is to serve the collective interests of their members. Collective goals take the form of collective public goods.

Collective goods are such that they cannot be withheld from any member of the eligible class, even noncontributors, i.e., those who do not help to supply the good. Moreover, such goods, if they are supplied to one member of the class, can be supplied to others at little or no marginal cost. This definition is similar to that offered by Olson (1971: 5-6), who states, "One purpose . . . characteristic of most organizations . . . is the furtherance of the interests of their members." Furthermore, he argues, "[T]heir characteristic and primary function is to advance the common interests of groups of individuals."[8]

A political organization, for purposes of this study, is an organization which seeks to further the common interests of its members through the provision of public goods, although the organization may also engage in activities peripheral to the supply of public goods. It should also be noted that, in this study, public goods need not be purely collective even though Olson (1971: 14) defines them as such. He does, however, point out (1971: 14 n. 21) that they may be collective only to a specific group. That is, the range of their collectivity may be limited.[9]

Public goods may be either tangible, such as roads and bridges, or intangible, such as a new president or an honest congress. Stokey and Zeckhauser (1978: 306-309) list three essential attributes of public goods. First, there will be under-provision of public goods since individuals lack an incentive to supply the goods themselves. Second, public goods exhibit nonrivalry in consumption; i.e., one actor's consumption of the good does not diminish another's. Finally, public goods are non-excludable. That is, noncontributors cannot be excluded from consuming the good. This last characteristic may not be intended, but it is usually impractical to exclude noncontributors. Of the three factors, Stokey and Zeckhauser (1978: 307) argue that nonrivalry is the most important. They also point out that the "publicness" of goods is a matter of degree. There are very few purely public goods.

Transnational terrorist groups are political organizations because they seek to provide public goods. A new regime, a Palestinian homeland, an independent Northern Ireland, release of certain prisoners, an Islamic revolution, among other goals, are examples of public goods sought by transnational terrorist groups. Ransom for hostages, depending upon the use to which the money is put, may or may not be a public good.

It should be noted that public goods may provide positive or negative utility. Presumably, those who favor the provision of the goods will derive some measure of positive utility from their provision. Those who oppose their provision will derive negative utility. Still others may be indifferent to some public goods. For example, if Northern Ireland becomes independent or is merged with Eire, many if not most Roman Catholics will derive positive utility while the Protestants will derive negative utility. Barring a unanimous opinion, there are both winners and losers in the provision of any public good.

There is yet another way in which terrorist groups can be considered political organizations. Terrorist groups may produce externalities which affect other members of society. Externalities can result from the provision of the public good itself. For example, if Northern Ireland becomes independent and a Catholic regime takes over which oppresses the Protestants, then the Protestants will suffer from the actions of the Catholic regime which they cannot control. Externalities can also result from the actions taken by a terrorist group in pursuit of a public good. If terrorists bomb a bus station, for example, those injured and killed will experience negative utility from the actions of the terrorists over which they have no control. Externalities, as noted earlier, occur when an actor is affected by the actions of others over which he has no control.

Transnational terrorist groups are political organizations. They do differ in some ways from ordinary interest groups, such as the American Conservative Union or Americans for Democratic Action, in the methods they use to attempt to provide public goods. Terrorist groups use political violence, terrorism. Ordinary interest groups generally, though not exclusively, use more peaceful activities such as lobbying, campaign contributions, letter writing, etc. Violence is not, however, unknown among ordinary interest groups, and terrorist groups may also engage in other, legitimate forms of political activity, as noted earlier.

Group Size, Coalitions, and Terrorism

Most theories of political interest groups are concerned with how those groups operate within the democratic process. Thus, there is no perfect correspondence between theories of interest groups and the study of transnational terrorism. Nonetheless, since both types of groups have a similar goal, i.e., the provision of public goods, the internal dynamics of the groups should be similar. There are some differences, however. Ordinary interest groups in Western society usually have some form of a democratic decision-making system. The decision-making systems utilized by terrorist groups remain largely unknown. Whatever type of internal decision-making system is used, several variables are likely to influence the transnational terrorist act. The size of the acting group and the presence of terrorist coalitions are among the influential variables.

Olson and Zeckhauser (1966: 267-268) argue that if the good sought by the group is purely public and collective the actions of any group member to supply the good will benefit all members. Therefore, in a large group, where any one member's fraction of the total benefit is small, no member has an incentive to contribute to the supply of the good since he will benefit from its supply whether he contributes or not.

Riker (1962), in his discussion of coalitions, also deals with the size of the group.[10] He states his basic axiom (Riker, 1962: 32): "In n-person, zero-sum games, where side payments are permitted, where players are rational, and where they have perfect information, only minimum winning coalitions will occur." Simply stated, Riker's axiom is that each member added to the winning group reduces the benefit available to the other members. Each additional member's support must also be purchased and therefore adds to the decision-making costs of the group as well.[11] Riker (1962: 32-33) goes on to argue that, in social situations, coalitions will be just large enough to satisfy some subjective probability of winning since perfect information is rarely available.

Since political organizations seek public goods it is possible

for a member to consume a good without making a contribution to its supply.[12] Large groups, therefore, must provide selective incentives or coercion, when possible, consisting of positive inducements or negative sanctions, apart from the public
goods themselves, in order to induce members of the benefit-
ting group to participate in the supply of the public goods by
making a contribution. Selective incentives must only be
available to those who formally join the organization and make
a contribution (Olson, 1971: 14-16). It is possible in this formulation for selective incentives to attract members to the
group who are indifferent or conceivably opposed to the public
goods which the group seeks.

Small groups differ from large groups in that they may be
able to supply a public good without selective incentives or
formal coercion. Face-to-face interaction between group members, larger individual benefit shares, and the possibility that
one individual's benefit share will be large enough to induce
him to supply the good by himself make small groups more
efficient at supplying a sufficient amount of public goods to
satisfy all members (Olson, 1971: 33-35). Intermediate groups,
which are between large and small groups in terms of size, operate through strategic interaction. Intermediate groups must
still be small enough so that the actions of one member have
a discernible effect on the other members (Olson, 1971: 49-50).
Small groups thus operate through face-to-face interaction,
intermediate groups through strategic interaction, and large
groups through selective incentives or coercion.

Olson (1971: 35) states that the larger the group, the less
optimal the supply of public goods will be. Since small groups
are better able to further their common interests than are large
groups, according to Olson, large groups often use small groups,
i.e., committees or the group's leadership, to make decisions
for the group as a whole (Olson, 1971: 52-53).

Olson (1971: 48) lists three factors which prevent large groups
from being able to further the common interests of their members:

1. The larger the group the smaller the fraction of the total benefit
   available to any single member. Since his fraction of the benefit is

small, a member has little incentive to make a contribution to the supply of a public good.

2. The larger the group the less likely it is that any one member or group of members will derive a sufficient benefit to supply the public good for the entire group.

3. The larger the group the larger the organizational costs.

Large groups, therefore, can only induce contributions through coercion or selective incentives, economic or social (Olson, 1971: 51). Social incentives, however, are also likely to be more effective in small groups than in large groups. In small groups face-to-face contact occurs among members. Peer pressure and moral persuasion will thus be more effective in inducing contributions from members of small groups than from members of large groups (Olson, 1971: 62). This is similar to Riker's (1962: 51) argument that in small groups considerations of loyalty and solidarity may dominate considerations for maximum victory. Riker (1962: 65) goes on to argue that the larger the group the less likely there is to be agreement on preferences among all members and states: "[A]s long as two conflicting interests remain in the party, neither can be satisfied."

Similar propositions regarding traditional alliances (formal coalitions of states) are developed by Holsti, Hopmann, and Sullivan (1973). They argue (1973: 6) that alliances will increase in size only to the point where they satisfy some subjective probability of winning. They also argue (1973: 54) that ideological heterogeneity and conflicting interests among members will impair the performance of an alliance. They contend further (1973: 29) that alliances formed for offensive purposes are short-lived.

Mickolus (1981: 5.69-5.70) gives three reasons why terrorist coalitions are difficult to organize successfully:

1. *Quid pro quo* arrangements must be met if the coalition is to succeed.

2. Personality and ideological clashes are likely to occur in coalitions.

3. The formation of a coalition requires that more people be made

aware of the plans, resources, and membership of a group. Coalitions, therefore, pose a greater security risk than do single group actions.

Coalitions of terrorist groups have problems similar to large groups if the above statements are correct. Based on this discussion and the review of previous literature on the subject, a number of propositions can be developed relating to the role of the size of the acting group and the presence of coalitions at the operational level of the transnational terrorist act. These propositions are outlined in the next section.

It should be noted that it is possible to develop many propositions about these two variables; however, this work develops only a limited number of such hypotheses which can be investigated with current data. Because data-gathering techniques for the study of transnational terrorism are imperfect, the results reported in Chapters 3 and 4 must be regarded as tentative rather than conclusive. Moreover, the current data available cover the period from 1968 through 1977. Nonetheless, with the provision that it must be regarded as tentative, this work presents a first empirical look at the role of the size of the acting group and the presence of coalitions as key variables in the transnational terrorist act.

TESTABLE PROPOSITIONS

Propositions about Group Size

It has been argued by some authors that terrorist groups tend to use only a limited number of tactics. Simple hit-and-run techniques, e.g., bombings, are the most common. These techniques may be used frequently because they are simple acts logistically and require only a small number of operatives. It can be argued that logistical requirements differ for different types of acts and that the size of the group will vary according to the type of act committed. Specifically, more difficult acts will require a larger group. This leads to the first hypothesis.

H1.1 The more difficult the act is logistically, the larger the group required to carry out the act. Simple acts will be carried out by smaller groups than moderately difficult acts, and moderately difficult acts will be carried out by a smaller group than difficult acts.

The data contains 22 different types of terrorist acts. Excluding events occurring only once, threats, hoaxes, conspiracies, and acts of an unknown type, the types of acts can be grouped as follows:

1. Simple acts. Bombings (all types), sniping, theft or break-in, sabotage, and shoot-outs with police.
2. Moderately difficult. Armed attacks (with missiles or other weapons), hijacking, and takeovers of non-aerial transports.
3. Difficult. Kidnapping, barricade and hostage, and facility occupation.

Some further clarification of this hypothesis can be offered at this point. The classification of the above types of acts is based on the amount of planning and resources which each type of action would normally entail. Difficult acts require the most of these commodities, simple acts the least. This determination is admittedly, like much of social science data, imperfect. There are no measures available on which this determination can be made. Therefore, one is forced to rely on appearances and introspection.

It has been asserted by some authors that a terrorist group uses only a limited number of tactics. It has a characteristic mode of operation. It can be argued that the size of the acting group is another characteristic of the specific group. This leads to the next hypothesis.

H1.2 The average size of the acting group will vary from one terrorist organization to another.

The testing of H1.2 will be done by comparing the average group size of groups active enough to have established a characteristic pattern of operation during the period covered by the data. While determining the exact level of activity necessary is basically an intuitive process, this hypothesis is tested by comparing groups that committed at least 40 acts of transnational terrorism during the period covered by the data and for whom the group size is known in ten or more cases. Ten cases is the minimum selected, although it would obviously be better to have a much larger number. However, since this is not possible, the hypothesis is tested using available data. The groups included and their frequency of activity are listed below:

1. Ejercito Revolucionario del Pueblo (ERP) (57)
2. Irish Republican Army-Provisional Wing (IRA) (211)
3. Popular Front for the Liberation of Palestine (PFLP) (79)
4. Black September Organization (BSO) (137)

The above hypothesis requires further elucidation. Obviously, there is nothing inherent in the fact that there are a variety of terrorist groups which would lead to variation in tactics or group size. The groups used for comparison are really surrogate variables. There are individual characteristics in each of the groups which lead to variation in group size. Since we do not, at this point, know enough about the organizational characteristics of groups to know what might result in these differences, group names are used to substitute for these characteristics. When more information is available on enough groups it may be possible, at that time, to determine whether the goals, ideology, decision-making structures, or other variables are responsible for variation in the size of the acting group.

Large groups are, according to Olson (1971), less capable of collective action than are small groups. This may be one reason why acting terrorist groups tend to be small.[13] Several factors will make large terrorist groups less successful than small terrorist groups. Large groups have more organizational problems, increased chances of internal dissension, and an increased security risk. This leads to hyopthesis H1.3.

H1.3 Large acting groups of terrorists will be less likely than normal sized groups to complete a terrorist act, i.e., commit a successful act.

A successful act is defined here as an act which is logistically complete, whether the group gained concessions or not.

It simply means that the terrorists were able to carry out the act and were not stopped before the act was complete. The exact classification of complete and incomplete acts is discussed later in this chapter.

A large group, since the acting group usually is quite small, will be defined as any group of seven or more acting terrorists. A normal group is simply one which falls within the usual size range for acting groups. Obviously, most groups will fall into the normal category. Large groups are taken to be only the top 15 percent of all groups in terms of size.[14] In the data there are 2,711 completed terrorist acts and 578 acts stopped at the scene, begun but not completed, or stopped at the planning stage.

When certain types of terrorist acts occur, negotiation takes place between the terrorists and the authorities. A peaceful end to a negotiated act requires agreement between the terrorists and the authorities and also requires internal agreement within the terrorist group. The larger the terrorist group, the less chance it will have of reaching internal agreement, i.e., the larger the group, the more heterogenous it is likely to be in terms of individual preferences (Mickolus, 1981: 5.69). It is, therefore, less likely that a negotiated act committed by a large group can be ended peacefully. This suggests several testable hypotheses.

H1.4 Large group, negotiated acts are more likely to end in violence than are small group acts and, therefore, large group acts are more likely to result in participants (terrorists, police, hostages, etc.) being killed than are small group events.

H1.5 through H1.8 are stated separately and tested individually. They are, however, closely related to H1.4 and can be considered as corollaries of that hypothesis since if H1.4 is not borne out by the data, it is unlikely that the others will be.

H1.5 The larger the group involved in a negotiated act, the greater the number of deaths resulting.

H1.6 Participants are more likely to be wounded during large group negotiated acts than during small group acts.

H1.7 The larger the group involved in a negotiated act, the higher the number of wounded participants.

H1.8 Large group, negotiated acts are more likely than small group acts to result in property damage.

Internal and external bargaining can only take place during negotiated terrorist acts. Therefore, in the test of this hypothesis, hit-and-run terrorist acts are not included. Negotiated acts include kidnapping, facility occupation, barricade and hostage episodes, hijacking, and the takeover of non-aerial transports.

If terrorist groups do indeed cooperate with one another and imitate one another, it is likely that across time more difficult types of acts would become more prevalent. These acts would require a larger group than simple acts. This leads to hypothesis H1.9.

H1.9 Across time, during the period from 1968 to 1977, the average size of the acting group will increase from year to year.

Obviously, time is not the actual cause of the change implied in H1.9. Time is used as a surrogate variable for changes in the environment within which terrorists operate. For example, as time progresses, transportation and communication systems may be improved, thus allowing closer cooperation among terrorist groups. The expected change in group size is due to these types of changes and not to the progression of time itself.

It has been suggested in the literature that different geographic regions are subject to particular types of acts and that cooperation among groups is a regional phenomenon. Terrorists within a given region are more likely to imitate each other in terms of tactics. Tactics, in this sense, would include characteristic group size.

Group size is likely to vary from region to region for several reasons. Specific groups may operate in a given region and their characteristic group size will affect the regional average. Terrorist organizations may also have an easier time recruiting operatives in some regions of the world where conditions make other means of redress impossible. However, a truly efficient authoritarian regime may be successful in preventing terrorist recruitment. The population of an area may affect the ability of terrorist organizations to recruit large numbers of operatives. Finally, in areas where ideology, religion, ethnicity, or some other characteristic is the basis for the polarization of the population, terrorist organizations may be able to recruit larger numbers of new members.

H1.10 The average size of the acting group will vary from one region of the world to another.

The literature also suggests that coalitional acts often involve one group assisting another group in the commission of an act which the latter group could not commit on its own. This suggests hypothesis H1.11.

H1.11 The average size of the acting group will be larger for coalitional groups than for single group acts.

Propositions about Coalitions

Mickolus (1981: 5.69) argues that cooperating terrorist groups must negotiate *quid pro quo* arrangements. Riker (1962: 65) argues that organizations containing competing interests are not likely to succeed. These arguments suggest the first hypothesis regarding terrorist coalitions.

H2.1 Coalitions are less likely to be able to commit a complete terrorist act than are single groups.

Aside from the necessary *quid pro quo* arrangements, Mickolus (1981: 5.70) argues that coalitions are likely to incur ideological or personality clashes. It is expected, therefore, that during negotiated acts there are likely to be internal disputes between the terrorist groups. Thus, a peaceful resolution is less likely during coalitional acts than during single group acts. This suggests several hypotheses.

H2.2 There are more likely to be participants killed during coalitional acts than during single group acts.

H2.3 through H2.6 are stated separately and are tested individually. However, as was the case with H1.5 through H1.8, they may be characterized as corollaries because if H2.2 is untrue, it is unlikely that H2.3 through H2.6 are true.

H2.3 The average number of deaths resulting from coalitional negotiated acts will be higher than for single group acts.

H2.4 Participants are more likely to be wounded during negotiated coalitional acts than during single group acts.

H2.5 The average number of participants wounded during coalitional acts will be higher than that for single group events.

H2.6 Coalitional acts are more likely to result in property damage than are single group events.

Mickolus (1982: 17), among others, argues that cooperation among terrorist groups is becoming increasingly frequent. If this is the case, then the data should verify the following hyopthesis.

H2.7 Coalitional acts as a percentage of all transnational terrorist acts will increase over the period of 1968 through 1977.

Originally, it was supposed on an intuitive basis that coalitions would be limited to committing terrorist acts with simple logistical requirements. This was supposed because coalitions face greater command and organizational difficulties than do single groups. However, a review of the literature led to a change in expectations regarding the behavior of coalitions. The literature suggests that coalitions usually are formed by one group helping another to commit an act which the latter group could not carry out on its own. That is, one group uses its resources to give another group the ability to carry out an act which is logistically too difficult for one group alone. This reconsideration leads to the next hypothesis.

H2.8 Coalitions are more likely than are single groups to commit logistically difficult terrorist acts.

Cooperation among terrorists has been argued by some scholars to be a phenomenon which occurs mainly at the re-

gional level. In some regions groups will cooperate more closely than in others. This suggests the next hypothesis.

H2.9 The frequency of coalitional activities will vary from one region to another.

Holsti, Hopmann, and Sullivan (1973: 29) argue that offensive alliances will disintegrate quickly. Terrorist coalitions are basically offensive alliances. This suggests the next hypothesis.

H2.10 Most terrorist coalitions will be of short duration.

Two groups will commit only a small number of coalitional acts together. Specifically, most coalitions will consist of only a single act.

Hypothesis H2.10 suggests that most terrorist coalitions will be of short duration. Nonetheless, there may occasionally be instances in which coincidence of interest or restraints imposed by resources may result in the formation of working partnerships between two groups of terrorists. A working partnership is defined here as four or more coalitional acts by the same groups. This leads to the final hypothesis.

H2.11 Some terrorist groups will form working partnerships.

Strictly speaking, this hypothesis cannot be verified. It is, however, possible to determine whether or not working partnerships did occur during the period covered by the data and to identify those partnerships which did occur.

In this section 22 specific hypotheses have been developed which are designed to guide an empirical study of the role of terrorist coalitions and the size of the acting group as key variables in the transnational terrorist act. These are two key organizational variables which are expected to affect the behavior of most political organizations. It is, however, fair to ask why these specific variables were chosen. There are three major reasons for this selection. First, there is a wide range of organizational variables that may have an impact on the transnational terrorist act. However, it is virtually impossible to study them all at one time. Therefore, two of these variables were selected. Second, these two variables are key variables in the sense that they may be expected to have an impact on any political organization. Third, current data on transnational terrorism contains only a limited number of organizational variables. The data is available to study these two variables. Information on some other organizational variables, such as decision-making and leadership, is not available in sufficient quantity or variety to carry out a meaningful empirical study.

THE DATA

The ITERATE Data Set

The data used in this study are from the 1982 revised version of the ITERATE data set (ITERATE2) constructed by Mickolus; they consist of transnational terrorist acts for the years 1968 through 1977.[15] It is made available in machine-readable format by the Inter-University Consortium for Political and Social Research (ICPSR) in Ann Arbor, Michigan.

The ITERATE data set is divided into four files. The first file, the common file, contains data on various attributes of transnational terrorist events. The second file contains data on the fate of the acting terrorists. The third file contains data on the fate of the involved hostages. The last file contains data on skyjacking events only. This study uses the common file which contains 38 variables and 3,329 cases. The other files contain only limited information and smaller numbers of cases. Allowing for missing cases, the other three files have insufficient information to be useful for testing the hypotheses under consideration. The other three files are also more specialized and do not contain the variables necessary for the testing of the hypotheses developed in Chapter 2.

The data set contains data on 1,884 single group events and 111 coalitional events. The number of groups is unknown in 1,334 cases. The 111 coalitional acts include 86 cases involving two groups, 16 cases involving three groups, and nine cases involving four groups.

The size of the acting group ranges from one, for which there are 290 cases, to more than 90. There are 2,560 cases for which the size of the group is unknown. The usable data set for group size consists of 769 cases.

The major problem with the testing of the hypotheses appears to be the possibility of a large number of missing cases for some variables. This could conceivably make some tests difficult. However, the data base contains a sufficient number of cases so that, even allowing for missing values, sufficient cases remain so that testing is possible. An assumption is also made, since there is no evidence to the contrary, that the missing data are randomly distributed, i.e., that no systematic error exists. If systematic errors do exist, for example if all the values on a particular variable are wrong, the tests utilizing that variable would be meaningless. Essentially, systematic error would invalidate any test using the variable on which the error occurred.

This research is an effort to test a theoretical understanding of terrorism using available data. Thus far, data collection efforts have been concerned mainly with tracking the trends of transnational terrorism and developing chronologies. Little theoretical work has informed data collection efforts. On the other hand, most theoretical treatments use no data. The rational choice studies, for example, develop deductive models and derive their conclusions through a logical process. Data, if used at all, are mainly anecdotal. This study attempts to provide a step towards correcting these shortcomings.

Future efforts may produce better data collection methods. For now, however, the best effort must be made using the available data. It should also be noted that imperfect data are not an unusual phenomenon in social science research. This observation does not mitigate against the need for data analysis on this subject. It does, however, point out the need to be aware of the limitations which current data place on empirical studies of terrorism.

This study proceeds by means of the normal hypothesis-testing sequence. Each of the hypotheses developed in the previous chapter is tested using the best appropriate available technique for the data involved.

Variables Used in the Study

A complete description of all the variables in the ITERATE data base can be found in Mickolus (1982). In this section a brief description of the variables not described in the previous section is presented.

The size of the group is the first key variable. It is measured on a ratio level scale ranging from one to 90 or more. For hypotheses which require a recoding of this variable, a normal or small terrorist group consists of six or fewer terrorists (669 cases), while a large group consists of seven or more terrorists (100 cases).

In order to test for more subtle differences in the data, a second recode scheme is used. In this second breakdown, groups are divided into one of four types: single actors (one person, 290 cases), small groups (two to five persons, 352 cases), intermediate groups (six to ten persons, 74 cases), and large groups (more than ten persons, 53 cases). Most hypotheses are tested using both the two-way classification and the four-way classification.[16]

The determination of where to divide the groups into size categories obviously is largely an intuitive process. Those who treat the size of the group as a key variable (e.g., Olson, 1971) do not define sizes explicitly. The sizes are relative to the distribution of the particular type of group. In this case, single actors, since they may be fundamentally different than a group, even a small one, are included as a separate category. Small groups include those groups up to the mean size of acting groups (which is actually 4.4). Intermediate groups include the next 10 percent of all groups. Large groups include only the top 7 percent of all groups. The cutoff point for large groups is simply all those larger than the other categories. While these categories are based partly on introspection, they are not unreasonable given that most acting groups are very small.

The second key variable in the study, coalitions, is defined as two or more groups acting together (111 cases), while single group events require only one group (1,884 cases).

The data set contains 22 different types of terrorist events. These have been recoded for some hypotheses into simple, moderately difficult, and difficult terrorist acts. For certain other hypotheses they are divided into negotiated and nonnegotiated acts. Hoaxes, threats, and conspiracies are excluded, as are event types which occur only once. Simple acts, as previously defined, constitute 2,438 cases. Moderately difficult acts include 251 cases. Difficult acts include 306 cases. Negotiated acts, as previously defined, constitute 404 cases with the remainder being nonnegotiated.

The groups used for intergroup comparisons have already been identified. Complete terrorist acts constitute 2,711 cases while 578 cases were incomplete.

Participants dead and participants wounded are measured on a ratio level scale. The number killed ranges from zero to 100. The number wounded ranges from zero to 300. There were 2,798 cases in which no participants were wounded and 2,924 cases in which no participants were killed. Participants were wounded in 531 cases and killed in 405.

Property damage does not include stolen property, ransom, or personal injury. There were 1,778 cases in which property damage occurred and 1,413 cases in which it did not.

To test hypotheses dealing with trends across time, comparisons are made from year to year. The years covered by the data are 1968 through 1977. There were 123 acts in 1968, 179 in 1969, 344 in 1970, 301 in 1971, 480 in 1972, 340 in 1973, 425 in 1974, 342 in 1975, 455 in 1976, and 340 in 1977.

Regional variation can be studied by recoding the location in which an incident began. For determining the regions, the pattern used by Mickolus (1977c: 217-221) is followed with some minor exceptions. Locations in the ITERATE data set which do not appear in Mickolus (1977c) have been coded here, and North America is treated as a separate region, not as part of the Atlantic Community. The regions coded are defined below along with their frequencies.

1. North America: 390 cases. United States, Canada, and Puerto Rico.
2. Latin America: 828 cases. Bahamas, Cuba, Haiti, Dominican Republic, Jamaica, Trinidad and Tobago, Barbados, Mexico, Guatemala, Honduras, El Salvador, Nicaragua, Costa Rica, Panama, Colombia, Venezuela, Ecuador, Peru, Brazil, Bolivia, Paraguay, Chile, Argentina, Uruguay.
3. Western Europe: 1,143 cases. United Kingdom, Northern Ireland, Eire, Netherlands, Belgium, Corsica, France, Switzerland, Spain, Portugal, West Germany, Italy, Austria, Vatican City, Greece, Cyprus, Finland, Sweden, Norway, Denmark.
4. Eastern Europe: 29 cases. Poland, Hungary, Yugoslavia, Bulgaria, Union of Soviet Socialist Republics (USSR).[17]
5. Africa: 104 cases. Mauritania, Ivory Coast, Sierra Leone, Ghana, Chad, Zaire, Uganda, Kenya, Tanzania, Zanzibar, Burundi, Somalia, French Somaliland, Ethiopia, Eritrea, Angola, Mozambique, Zambia, Zimbabwe, South Africa, Lesotho, Botswana.
6. Middle East: 494 cases. Morocco, Canary Islands, Spanish Sahara, Algeria, Tunisia, Libya, Sudan, Iran, Turkey, Iraq, Egypt, Syria, Lebanon, Jordan, Israel, Saudi Arabia, Yemen, Kuwait, Bahrain, Dubai, Abu Dhabi, United Arab Emirates (UAR).
7. Asia: 314 cases. Afghanistan, People's Republic of China (PRC), Taiwan (ROC), Hong Kong, South Korea, Japan, India, Bangladesh, Pakistan, Burma, Nepal, Sri Lanka, Thailand, Kampuchea, Laos, Malaysia, Singapore, Philippines, Indonesia, Australia, New Zealand.

It should be noted that not every possible location has been coded or included in the above list. Only those locations where an act of transnational terrorism occurred which is recorded in the data set are included. This does not mean that other locations are not subject to transnational terrorism. Acts have occurred after 1977, of course, and it is also possible that many other countries not subject to transnational terrorism may nevertheless have significant frequencies of domestic terrorism.

It should also be noted that some of the locations in the above data set are nation-states while others are subnational localities. Certain subnational localities are coded separately in order to facilitate their location for research on transnational terrorism in the location involved. For example, even though

Northern Ireland is part of the United Kingdom, transnational terrorism in Northern Ireland alone may be of interest to some researchers who are unconcerned about the rest of the United Kingdom.

Two variables, duration of coalition and presence of a working partnership, depend upon the number of times that two terrorist groups work together in the commission of acts of terrorism. The data set includes the identification of two groups per coalitional act. Working partnerships and coalition duration are investigated by studying the frequency with which pairs of groups act together.

A description of every variable in the data set is not offered here because such a description is available in Mickolus (1982). In this section an effort has been made to describe the variables necessary for testing the hypotheses developed in the previous section.

Limitations of the Data Base

There are some limitations of the ITERATE data base which should be pointed out. One difficulty is that there may be incomplete coverage of transnational terrorism in Eastern Europe.

A second limitation is that the data was collected only through 1977. It cannot be assumed that the behavior of the groups in the data set has been the same in the intervening seven years. Thus, data for later periods might supplement the findings presented here. It should not, however, be assumed that terrorist behavior has changed since that time. Nonetheless, some groups may have been behaving atypically during that period. The reader whose concern is with specific groups is urged to find as much information as he or she can regarding that group both before and after the period covered by the data set.

The final problem with the ITERATE data set is that it was not collected with a view toward organizational variables. Thus, while it is the best data set available, it is not designed specifically for this type of study. When a researcher has limited time and resources, it is often necessary to undertake a secondary analysis of existing data. This study is a secondary analysis.

As researchers begin to look more closely at the organizational variables affecting terrorism, better data may become available. Future data collection could focus on such variables as leadership styles, ideological variation, decision-making systems, and other organizational factors. Such data may not be easy to collect. A great deal is known about some groups and little is known about others. However, the effort may well prove to be worthwhile.

NOTES

1. Obviously, the findings of this study must be considered suggestive rather than final. It is impossible, for example, to know whether the increase in the number of terrorist events is due to an actual increase in activity or to improved reporting techniques. One cannot be certain that a data base really contains all possible cases. The other findings, e.g., those regarding the types of acts committed by terrorists, may be more reliable. Assuming that no particular type of event is overreported or underreported, the distribution of event types should approximate reality.

2. Gurr (1979) does not present a specific definition of what constitutes a political motive. He does, however, list seven types of political motives:

1) seize power, 2) oppose specific policies and actions, 3) oppose specific public figures, 4) oppose private political figures or groups, 5) oppose foreign government's policies, personnel, 6) several of the above, and 7) diffuse political purposes. (Gurr, 1979: Table 9, p. 39)

The last category is vague and consists of undescribed political purposes.

3. Ideally, an actor would know which action would lead to the preferred outcome, i.e., yield the highest utility. However, actors rarely have perfect information about the outcomes of each act and generally are uncertain about whether a given action will in fact lead to a given outcome. The actor must, therefore, estimate payoffs and probabilities of outcomes for any action.

There are problems associated with defining rationality as behavior in accordance with expected utility maximization. The major problem is that the definition of rationality is tautological. It rests on the axiom that people will behave in accordance with their preferences. Those preferences cannot usually be reliably determined except by observing the actor's behavior. Thus, whatever action is selected may be argued to be in accord with the actor's transitive preferences. It is not, strictly speaking, possible to demonstrate irrational behavior even where an actor's behavior is markedly deviant from that of other actors.

One can make a plausible argument that altruism is rational behavior. The argument is simply that a man must have preferred some altruistic behavior to selfish behavior or he would not have chosen it. Even behavior which society normally classifies as "crazy" can be defined as rational by this definition. One can plausibly argue that a man who climbs the library tower at the University of Texas and shoots passersby at random is rational. He must have preferred shooting people to other activities, e.g., playing Frisbee, or he would not have acted as he did.

It should be noted that rationality theory does not deal with the mental health of actors. It is not based on a social, moral, religious, or psychological understanding of how actors should behave. Rationality theory does not judge the preferred outcomes of actors. Society may determine how people ought to behave. Rationality, however, has nothing to do with this determination.

In many instances the costs of obtaining perfect or near-perfect information are prohibitive. In such cases an actor may make a conscious decision to act on imperfect information.

Thus, there are several reasons why an actor will choose the course of action which appears to offer the highest utility rather than the course which does in fact offer the highest utility. In other instances an actor may be forced to satisfice, i.e., choose an action which meets some minimum standard of expected utility.

What the rational choice model implies is basically that under conditions of perfect information, an actor will choose the alternative offering the highest utility. Under real conditions these assumptions must be relaxed. An actor will choose the action believed to be the best under the circumstances.

4. Externalities are defined by Stokey and Zeckhauser (1978: 303) simply as "situations in which the actions of one individual . . . affect the welfare of another." They are costs or benefits to one actor which result from the actions of another actor over which the first actor has no control.

5. Tullock (1972: Chapter 7) discusses the efficacy of voting, which is similar to participating in a revolution. Voting, and revolutionary activity, may have a negative utility to most actors. The efficacy of the action (E) is equal to the benefit (B) derived from one outcome as

opposed to another times the probability of the actor's participation making a difference (P) minus the costs of participation (C). Thus, efficacy can be calculated as $E = PB - C$. P in voting is equal to one divided by the number of voters. P is approximately zero in most cases. Thus, after the costs of participation are subtracted, efficacy may actually be negative. Participation in voting or revolution is often due to some reason other than efficacy. Ideology, for example, might lead an actor to join a revolution even though he knows that his participation will not be decisive.

6. Olson (1971) treats the free rider problem in some detail.

7. Surrogate states are states through which the support for terrorists is funneled. This allows the Soviet Union to channel resources to terrorist organizations and still maintain a plausible denial.

8. Olson's (1971) theory was a challenge to traditional pluralist theories of political interest groups. Olson's theory is a rational choice, social and economic exchange theory of interest groups. The merits of this particular viewpoint need not be fully debated here. However, the exchange theory of interest groups has been extended or modified by several scholars: Frohlich, Oppenheimer, and Young (1971); Dobson, Franke, and Jones (1981); Salisbury (1969); Moe (1980); and Oots (1983). The curious reader should consult these works. Rational choice as an approach to politics is given much broader coverage by Downs (1957) and Buchanan and Tullock (1965).

9. Buchanan (1968) offers a more complete discussion of types of public goods. It is not necessary to discuss the full range of divisibility or indivisibility of all types of public goods here. They may be indivisible over a limited range or may, like national defense, be indivisible over an entire nation. For discussions of various types of goods and their provision by interest groups, see Chamberlin (1974); Frohlich, Hunt, Oppenheimer, and Wagner (1975); and Frohlich and Oppenheimer (1970).

10. Riker (1962) deals with coalitions of individuals in social decision-making situations, not with coalitions of groups.

11. Buchanan and Tullock (1965: Chapter 6) also discuss the decision-making costs associated with the size of the group needed to make a decision.

12. Obviously, this is strictly true only for nonexclusionary public goods. If a good is nonexclusionary, there is no way to prevent any eligible member from consuming the good.

13. The acting group is the group which actually participates in the initiation of the terrorist action. Group size, for present purposes, is based on the acting group, not the entire terrorist organi-

zation. The acting group, which carries out the actions of the organization, fulfills a role similar to that which a committee performs for other large organizations. That is, a small group is used to do what it would be impossible for the entire organization to do collectively.

14. Because of the distribution of sizes, large groups actually only consist of the upper 13 percent of all acting groups, even though 15 percent was used as the cutoff point.

The group size data is, as is all data in this study, from the 1982 version of the ITERATE data set. Most of the data was collected from public sources, e.g., newspapers and government documents. Mickolus (1980) presents a complete list of all ITERATE data sources.

15. For a complete description of the data set, see the ITERATE codebook (Mickolus, 1982).

16. The size of the group includes only those involved in the initiation of the action. It does not include support personnel or other group members who may be involved in planning, etc.

17. As with many types of data from Eastern Europe, the small number of cases may represent incomplete reporting of terrorism in that region. There is no way to determine whether or not this is the case.

III

HYPOTHESIS TESTING I: GROUP SIZE

HYPOTHESIS 1.1

Three tests were performed for hypothesis H1.1: an analysis of variance (ANOVA) on group size with difficulty of the act as the independent variable, a crosstabulation of the two-way classification of group size by difficulty of the act, and a crosstabulation of the four-way group size classification by difficulty of the act. Hypothesis H1.1, as noted earlier, states that the more difficult the act of terrorism, the larger the terrorist group. Table 3.1 shows the results of the ANOVA for H1.1.

Table 3.1 demonstrates quite clearly that those acts designated as "difficult" do tend to be committed by a larger group than are simple acts. It is puzzling that simple acts do not have the smallest average group size. However, the difference between simple acts and moderately difficult acts is slight. The difference between difficult acts and both of the other categories is much larger. The data is generally supportive of H1.1. The F-value (8.85) is substantial. This finding may also be of some policy significance since it may, after further refinement, be possible to predict accurately the size of the terrorist group, given knowledge of the type of act which has taken place. Authorities might then have a better understanding of the manpower of their adversaries.

TABLE 3.1

ONE-WAY ANOVA: GROUP SIZE BY DIFFICULTY OF THE ACT

Difficulty	N	Mean Group Size
Simple	274	4.40
Moderately Difficult	166	4.11
Difficult	139	7.74

grand mean=5.12   F=8.85   p=.001   df= 2, 576   n=579

Mean square:
explained	633.11
residual	71.53
total	73.48

TABLE 3.2

CROSSTABULATION OF GROUP SIZE BY DIFFICULTY OF THE
TERRORIST ACT: TWO-WAY SIZE CLASSIFICATION

Size	Difficulty of Terrorist Act			
	Simple	Moderate	Difficult	Total
Normal	246 (89.8%) (50.4%)	143 (86.1%) (29.3%)	99 (71.2%) (20.3%)	488 (84.3%)
Large	28 (10.2%) (30.8%)	23 (13.9%) (25.3%)	40 (28.8%) (44.0%)	91 (15.7%)
Total	274 (47.3%)	166 (28.7%)	139 (24.0%)	579 (100%)

chi-square=24.58   df=2   p=.001

Table 3.2 shows the results of the crosstabulation of the two-way group size classification by difficulty of the act.

Table 3.2 presents additional evidence for H1.1. Large groups committed 28.8 percent of all difficult acts, versus 13.9 percent of moderately difficult acts, and 10.2 percent of all simple acts. Two other facets of terrorism are brought out by the table. The size of the acting group is generally small. The table shows that 84.3 percent of all acts were committed by a group of six or fewer terrorists. Large groups are comparatively rare.

It also indicates that simple terrorist acts make up the largest number of terrorist acts. As shown in the table, 47.3 percent of all acts were simple, 28.7 percent were moderately difficult, and only 24.0 percent were difficult acts.

Table 3.2 illustrates that the more difficult an act of terrorism is, the more likely it is to be committed by a large group. It also shows that large groups tend to specialize in difficult acts. For example, 44.0 percent of all large group acts were difficult, 25.3 percent were moderately difficult, and 30.8 percent were simple acts. Nonetheless, most acts, even difficult acts, are committed by small groups, i.e., six or fewer terrorists.

The data also tend to bear out the judgment that groups tend to specialize in particular types of acts. A group which is capable of organizing a large acting group would be more likely to commit a difficult act. The inability of many groups to organize a large acting group may be responsible, in part, for

TABLE 3.3

CROSSTABULATION OF GROUP SIZE BY DIFFICULTY OF THE TERRORIST ACT: FOUR-WAY SIZE CLASSIFICATION

Size	Difficulty of the Act			
	Simple	Moderate	Difficult	Total
Single Actor	99 (36.1%) (73.9%)	24 (14.5%) (17.9%)	11 (7.9%) (8.2%)	134 (23.1%)
Small	138 (50.4%) (42.1%)	112 (67.5%) (34.1%)	78 (56.1%) (23.8%)	328 (56.6%)
Intermediate	17 (6.2%) (24.3%)	24 (14.5%) (34.3%)	29 (20.9%) (41.4%)	70 (12.1%)
Large	20 (7.3%) (42.6%)	6 (3.6%) (12.8%)	21 (15.1%) (44.7%)	47 (8.1%)
Total	274 (47.3%)	166 (28.7%)	139 (24.0%)	579 (100%)

chi-square=74.87   df=6   p=.001

the fact that most terrorist acts are simple. This finding is only inference, since it cannot be demonstrated from the data.

Table 3.2 presents strong evidence for H1.1. The chi-square is significant at .001. There is a strong relationship between the difficulty of the act and the size of the acting group.

Table 3.3 presents the results of a crosstabulation of the four-way group size classification by difficulty of the act.

The chi-square for Table 3.3 is, again, highly significant. Table 3.3 presents further evidence for H1.1. Only 13.5 percent of the simple acts were committed by large or intermediate groups. However, large or intermediate groups committed 18.1 percent of all moderately difficult acts, and 36.0 percent of all difficult acts. The direction of the differences in the table is, for the most part, consistent with the hypothesis. If the percentage of acts classified as difficult is considered, the result is striking. Only 8.2 percent of single actor events were difficult, compared with 23.8 percent for small groups, 41.4 percent for intermediate groups, and 44.7 percent for large groups.

The evidence for H1.1 appears to be strong. All three tests of the hypothesis have failed to verify the null hypothesis.

HYPOTHESIS 1.2

Hypothesis H1.2, stated briefly, holds that the average size of the acting group will vary from one transnational terrorist organization to another. Four groups were used for comparison. The hypothesis was tested using an ANOVA on group size with the acting organization as the independent variable. The results of the ANOVA are shown in Table 3.4.

Hypothesis H1.2 is only partially borne out by the ANOVA in Table 3.4. There is a large difference between the ERP (Ejercito Revolucionario del Pueblo) and the other three organizations. Outside of this rather large difference, there appears to be virtually no difference among the organizations in terms of group size. The F-value is significant at slightly less than .05, and it does inspire some confidence in the hypothesis. Several factors could account for the lack of a more solid demonstration of this hypothesis.

Among the factors which may be partly responsible is the

TABLE 3.4

ONE-WAY ANOVA ON GROUP SIZE WITH ORGANIZATION INDEPENDENT

ORGANIZATION	N	MEAN GROUP SIZE
ERP	12	6.58
IRA	16	3.69
PFLP	41	3.22
BSO	33	3.70

grand mean=3.84 F=3.06 p=.032 df= 2, 98 n=102
Mean square:

explained	35.71
residual	11.68
total	12.31

fact that only four groups were chosen for study. This choice was necessary in order to obtain groups which were active enough to have established a characteristic pattern of behavior. Groups not included could have widely varying average group sizes. Secondly, for the ERP the group size was known in only 12 cases. It could be that one or more atypical cases occurred which pushed its average size out of line with the others. This problem raises another issue. Since it is difficult to get a large enough sample on some groups to establish a meaningful average group size, it may not be possible to study the characteristics of certain groups with confidence. That is, if one is interested solely in the behavior pattern of a single group, a lack of evidence is likely to hamper the study. Few groups committed enough acts during the period covered by the data to have established a characteristic pattern of behavior that could be studied empirically.

HYPOTHESIS 1.3

Hypothesis H1.3 states that large terrorist groups are less likely than their smaller counterparts to be able to commit a complete terrorist act. In order to test this hypothesis, cross-tabulations were performed using both the two-way and four-way group size classifications. The crosstabulation of whether the act was complete by the two-way group size classification is shown in Table 3.5.

Table 3.5 does not support the hypothesis that large groups are less successful than small groups at being able to commit a complete terrorist act. The table shows virtually no difference between normal groups and large groups. Most terrorist acts are carried to logistical completion regardless of the size of the acting group. It is possible that some subtle differences may have been missed by using only a two-way classification of group size. Therefore, Table 3.6 shows the results of a crosstabulation using the four-way group size classification.

Table 3.6 also contradicts H1.3. While there are differences in the table, and they are significant, it does not appear that large groups are less likely than small groups to commit a complete terrorist act. Small groups appear to be the least

TABLE 3.5 (a)

CROSSTABULATION OF COMPLETENESS BY GROUP SIZE:
TWO-WAY GROUP SIZE CLASSIFICATION

Completeness	Group Size		
	Normal	Large	Total
Incomplete	125 (18.7%) (87.4%)	18 (18.0%) (12.6%)	143 (18.6%)
Complete	544 (81.3%) (86.9%)	82 (82.0%) (13.1%)	626 (81.4%)
Total	669 (87.0%)	100 (13.0%)	769 (100%)

Z1=0.17   Z2=-0.17

[a]Z-scores are based on the difference of proportions test found in Blalock (1979: 232–234) and are derived by comparing the percentages in the first column with those in the second. For example, the percentages of complete and incomplete acts for normal and large groups were compared. The percentage of normal group acts which were incomplete is 18.7. The comparable percentage for large groups is 18.0. These percentages were then compared using the difference of proportions test. Z1 refers to the Z-score for the first row, Z2 to the score for the second row, and Z3 for the third row in all tables where the difference of proportions is reported.

TABLE 3.6

CROSSTABULATION OF COMPLETENESS BY GROUP SIZE:
FOUR-WAY SIZE CLASSIFICATION

Completeness	Group Size				
	Single Actor	Small Group	Intermediate Group	Large Group	Total
Incomplete	34 (11.7%) (23.8%)	86 (24.4%) (60.1%)	14 (18.9%) (8.8%)	9 (17.0%) (6.3%)	143 (18.6%)
Complete	256 (88.3%) (40.9%)	266 (75.6%) (42.5%)	60 (81.1%) (9.6%)	44 (83.0%) (7.0%)	626 (81.4%)
Total	290 (37.7%)	352 (45.8%)	74 (9.6%)	53 (6.9%)	769 (100%)

chi-square=17.06   df=3   p=.001

successful at being able to complete a terrorist act. This would indicate that larger groups are not under an increased security risk to the extent of being unable to carry an act to completion.

It is surprising that small groups should be the least successful. Olson's (1971) work led us to expect small groups to be the most successful at carrying out a complete act of terrorism. However, there are several possible reasons for this finding. Small groups may attempt to commit acts which they lack the resources to complete. Large groups could possibly have an advantage in that even if they do experience internal dissent, they may still have enough members after the dissenters have defected to be able to carry out the act. Defections from a smaller group may be more critical than those from a larger group. In any event, this finding remains somewhat puzzling and is contrary to what was expected under the assumption that Olson's (1971) postulates about large groups are correct.

HYPOTHESIS 1.4

Hypotheses H1.4, H1.5, H1.6, H1.7, and H1.8 are all related to the potential for damage or injury which results from a large

TABLE 3.7

CROSSTABULATION OF RESULTING DEATHS BY SIZE OF THE
ACTING GROUP: TWO-WAY SIZE CLASSIFICATION

Did Death Result?	Size of Group		
	Normal	Large	Total
No	141	35	176
	(78.3%)	(70.0%)	(76.5%)
	(80.1%)	(19.9%)	
Yes	39	15	54
	(21.7%)	(30.0%)	(23.5%)
	(72.2%)	(27.8%)	
Total	180	50	230
	(78.3%)	(21.7%)	(100%)

Z1=1.22   Z2=-1.22

group carrying out a negotiated act of terrorism. Only terrorist acts usually associated with negotiation were included in
testing this group of propositions. Hypothesis H1.4 states that
large group terrorist acts are more likely than other acts to
end in death for some participants. H1.4 was tested by cross-
tabulating whether or not deaths resulted from the terrorist
act by the size of the acting group, using both two-way and
four-way group size. Table 3.7 presents the first crosstabulation for H1.4.

The findings in Table 3.7 are only marginally supportive of
the hypothesis. The Z-scores are not significant. However, since
the critical value for a .10 probability for the difference of proportions test (one-tailed) is 1.29, they are very close. There does
appear to be a relationship, albeit not necessarily a strong one,
between group size and the probability of deaths occurring. It
can be seen that deaths occurred in 30.0 percent of the large
group acts versus only 21.7 percent of the normal group acts.

It is interesting to note that if large and normal groups are
compared on all acts, rather than only on negotiated acts,
deaths occur in 35.4 percent of the large group acts and 23.6
percent of the normal group acts. Large groups are somewhat
more likely to commit an act which ends in the death of one

TABLE 3.8

CROSSTABULATION OF WHETHER DEATH RESULTED BY THE SIZE OF THE
TERRORIST GROUP: FOUR-WAY SIZE CLASSIFICATION

Did Death Result?		Size of Group			
	Single Actor	Small Group	Intermediate Group	Large Group	Total
No	25 (86.2%) (14.2%)	106 (78.5%) (60.2%)	26 (60.5%) (14.8%)	19 (82.6%) (10.8%)	176 (76.5%)
Yes	4 (13.8%) (7.4%)	29 (21.5%) (53.7%)	17 (39.5%) (31.5%)	4 (17.4%) (7.4%)	54 (23.5%)
Total	29 (12.6%)	135 (58.7%)	43 (18.7%)	23 (10.0%)	230 (100%)

chi-square=8.46   df=3   p=.037

or more participants. Table 3.8 presents the crosstabulation of
death by group size for negotiated acts using the four-way group
size classification.

The table indicates that small and intermediate groups are
the most likely to commit terrorist acts which result in death.
This finding is contrary to expectations. However, it is possible that this finding corroborates Jenkins (1979: 5), who argues that small groups may be more influenced by the idiosyncracies of individual leaders or members. A small or
intermediate group, with one or two extremist members, may
be potentially more dangerous than a large group which di-
lutes the influence of radical individual members. Still, as might
be expected, small groups would be more deadly than intermediate groups. A plausible explanation can be offered for this
finding. An intermediate group is more likely than a small
group to contain a wide range of ideological orientations.
Therefore, extremist members are more likely to occur in intermediate or large groups. However, the large group can di-
lute the influence of the individual members so that the extremists have less influence on the outcome.

HYPOTHESIS 1.5

In order to test H1.5, that the larger the group the greater the number of resulting deaths, three tests were conducted. A Pearson product-moment correlation of number of deaths with number of terrorists in the acting group was performed. A t-test comparing the average number of deaths from normal and large groups was done. Finally, an ANOVA was carried out on the number of deaths by the four-way group size classification.

The correlation between group size and number of deaths ($-.03$, $p = .34$) does not support H1.5. It is insignificant and is contrary to the expected direction. Thus, the association between group size and number of deaths is virtually non-existent. The t-test resulted in marginally stronger findings. The average number of deaths for normal group acts was 1.24. For large group acts the mean was 2.78, with 228 degrees of freedom, $T = -1.19$ ($p = .117$, one-tailed). The significance level is not high for the t-test. However, it is clear that large group acts generally do result in a greater number of deaths than do normal group acts. The ANOVA results are presented in Table 3.9.

TABLE 3.9

ONE-WAY ANOVA: NUMBER OF DEATHS BY SIZE OF THE ACTING GROUP

Size	N	Mean Deaths
Single actor	29	3.59
Small group	135	0.66
Intermediate group	43	3.67
Large group	23	0.48

grand mean=1.57 F=2.32 p=.076 df= 3, 226 N=230

Mean square:
    explained 149.23
    residual   64.26
    total   65.37

Table 3.9 presents some interesting results, although they are not what was expected. Single actor and intermediate group events produce the largest number of deaths. Single actor events average 3.59 deaths per negotiated act while intermediate group events average 3.67. It is interesting to note that when all acts are included in the totals, single actors average only 0.95 and intermediate groups average 2.77. Large groups, however, have a mean of 1.02 over all acts while small groups average 0.91. It appears that when single actors or intermediate groups are involved, negotiated acts result in a higher number of deaths than other acts. Nonetheless, the findings in Table 3.9 require some explanation.

The most acceptable explanation seems again to be the greater influence extremist members may have on intermediate groups. Single actors, it appears, are less likely to accept a peaceful settlement to a negotiated act. It is possible that single actors are more likely to be extremists. A single actor who commits a negotiated terrorist act without the support of others must be highly ideological. Therefore, the political cause is more important than obtaining a peaceful settlement. It could be that there is a moderating trend in larger numbers.

HYPOTHESIS 1.6

Hypothesis H1.6 holds that large groups are more likely to commit negotiated terrorist acts which result in injury to participants. The same tests, substituting the number wounded for the number dead, were performed for H1.6 as for H1.4. Using the two-way group size classification, Table 3.10 presents the crosstabulation of whether participants were wounded.

Table 3.10 requires little explanation. It shows virtually no difference between large and normal terrorist groups. The second crosstabulation appears in Table 3.11.

Table 3.11 shows that intermediate groups are the most likely to commit a negotiated act that results in the wounding of participants. Small groups are the next most likely to carry out such an act. The probability for chi-square is .11. This is not highly significant. However, it does seem that intermedi-

TABLE 3.10

CROSSTABULATION OF WOUNDED BY GROUP SIZE:
TWO-WAY SIZE CLASSIFICATION

Were Participants Wounded?	Size of Group		
	Normal	Large	Total
No	132 (74.6%) (78.1%)	37 (74.0%) (21.9%)	169 (74.4%)
Yes	45 (25.4%) (77.6%)	13 (26.0%) (22.4%)	58 (25.6%)
Total	177 (78.0%)	50 (22.0%)	227 (100%)

Z1=.086   Z2=-.086

TABLE 3.11

CROSSTABULATION OF WOUNDED BY GROUP SIZE:
FOUR-WAY GROUP SIZE CLASSIFICATION

Were Participants Wounded?	Size of Group				
	Single Actor	Small Group	Intermediate Group	Large Group	Total
No	25 (86.2%) (14.8%)	98 (74.2%) (58.0%)	27 (62.8%) (16.0%)	19 (82.6%) (11.2%)	169 (74.4%)
Yes	4 (13.8%) (6.9%)	34 (25.8%) (58.6%)	16 (37.2%) (27.6%)	4 (17.4%) (6.9%)	58 (25.6%)
Total	29 (12.8%)	132 (58.1%)	43 (18.9%)	23 (10.1%)	227 (100%)

chi-square=5.99   df=3   p=.112

ate groups are far more likely than single actors or large groups to commit an act that results in persons being wounded. Small groups are not quite as likely to do so as are intermediate groups. The moderating influence of the larger group, again, seems to be a plausible explanation.

The fact that single actors were even less likely than large groups to commit acts which resulted in participants being wounded is surprising. Single actors were also unlikely to commit acts which ended in death for participants; however, their acts did result in a very high average number of deaths. It appears that when single actors committed acts which resulted in death, they killed large numbers of people. Nonetheless, it is difficult to explain why their frequencies of violent outcomes are very similar to those for large groups.

HYPOTHESIS 1.7

H1.7 is very similar to H1.5. It holds that the larger the acting group committing a negotiated terrorist act, the higher the number of wounded participants will be. Again, substituting the number wounded for the number killed, the same tests used for H1.5 were used for H1.7.

The Pearson product-moment for number of terrorists and number of wounded is very small, .03 (p = .327). The association between group size and number of participants wounded is very weak. The t-test shows that normal groups averaged 1.95 wounded per negotiated incident, while the mean for large groups was 3.18 (T = −1.03, df = 225, p = .152, one-tailed). While the T does not appear to be highly significant, it does seem that large group acts do result in more participants being wounded than do normal group acts. An average of 1.3 more participants are wounded during large group acts than during normal group acts. This is a substantial number of wounded actors, even if it is not highly significant statistically.

Table 3.12 presents the results of the ANOVA performed to test H1.7. The F-value for Table 3.12 is not very high and the statistical significance of the differences found in the table is slight. Nonetheless, the table generally supports the findings

TABLE 3.12

ONE-WAY ANOVA: NUMBER WOUNDED BY SIZE OF THE ACTING GROUP

Size	N	Mean Wounded
Single Actor	29	1.24
Small Group	132	1.91
Intermediate Group	43	4.16
Large Group	23	1.65

grand mean=2.22 F=1.27 df= 3, 227 p=.284 N=227

Mean square:
explained	70.08
residual	55.05
total	55.25

of previous tests in this study; i.e., intermediate groups have
the highest mean number of wounded participants. This time,
however, single actors have the smallest average. The same
explanation offered previously for intermediate groups is ap-
plicable here. As for single actors, they remain a puzzle at this
point. The results on single actors for H1.5 and H1.7 are contradictory. The cause of these discrepancies is unknown.

HYPOTHESIS 1.8

H1.8 is similar to H1.4 and H1.6 in that it holds that property damage is more likely to occur during large group negotiated acts than during normal group negotiated acts. Two
crosstabulations, using two-way and four-way group size classifications, were performed on whether property damage occurred. Table 3.13 shows the results of the two-way crosstabulation.

Table 3.13 provides only weak evidence for the hypothesis.
The Z-scores are slightly less than what is required for a one-
tailed probability of .10. It does show, however, that large
groups were more likely, but not much, to commit an act of
terrorism which resulted in property damage than were nor-

TABLE 3.13

CROSSTABULATION OF PROPERTY DAMAGE BY GROUP SIZE:
TWO-WAY SIZE CLASSIFICATION

Did Damage Occur?	Size of Group		
	Normal	Large	Total
Yes	22 (12.8%) (68.8%)	10 (20.0%) (21.3%)	32 (14.4%)
No	150 (87.2%) (78.9%)	40 (80.0%) (21.1%)	190 (85.6%)
Total	172 (77.5%)	50 (22.5%)	222 (100%)

$Z1 = -1.26$ $Z2 = 1.26$

mal sized groups. Table 3.14 shows the crosstabulation using the four-way group size classification.

Again, the chi-square is not significant. However, the percentage of negotiated acts resulting in property damage increases in a linear fashion as group size increases. Although the number of cases for some categories is small, it does appear that large group negotiated acts do result in property damage more frequently than do acts committed by smaller groups. This is probably for the reason stated in Chapter 2: the larger the group, the less likely it is to reach internal consensus and, therefore, the less likely it is to accept a peaceful negotiated settlement. The significance of this finding is discussed further in the last two chapters.

HYPOTHESIS 1.9

Hypothesis H1.9 holds that the average group size should increase over the period from 1968 to 1977. Two tests were performed on this hypothesis. First, an ANOVA on group size by year was performed. Secondly, a t-test was done which compared the average group size for the first half of the pe-

TABLE 3.14

CROSSTABULATION OF PROPERTY DAMAGE BY GROUP SIZE: FOUR-WAY GROUP SIZE CLASSIFICATION

Did Damage Occur?	Size of Group				
	Single Actor	Small Group	Intermediate Group	Large Group	Total
Yes	2 (6.9%) (6.3%)	17 (13.4%) (53.1%)	8 (18.6%) (25.0%)	5 (21.7%) (15.6%)	32 (14.4%)
No	27 (93.1%) (14.2%)	110 (86.6%) (57.9%)	35 (81.4%) (18.4%)	18 (78.3%) (9.5%)	190 (85.6%)
Total	29 (13.1%)	127 (57.2%)	43 (19.4%)	23 (10.4%)	222 (100%)

chi-square=3.05   df=3   p=.384

TABLE 3.15

ONE-WAY ANOVA: GROUP SIZE BY YEAR

Year	N	Mean Size
1968	31	4.32
1969	54	2.93
1970	106	4.54
1971	85	3.60
1972	82	4.01
1973	85	3.91
1974	82	3.37
1975	75	5.76
1976	92	4.89
1977	77	5.83

grand mean=4.35 F=1.12 df= 9, 759 p=.348 N=769

Mean square:
        explained   67.96
        residual   60.85
        total   60.93

riod with that for the second half. Table 3.15 presents the AN-OVA results.

The results shown in Table 3.15 are not totally supportive of the hypothesis. There are differences from year to year; however, there is no linear increase in group size. It is interesting that the last three years all have high mean group sizes in comparison with most other years. The years 1975 and 1977 have particularly high means. The evidence is ambiguous in Table 3.15, and the differences that appear are not significant. The data do not support H1.9.

When the period was divided into halves, the first half had a mean group size of 3.93, while the second half averaged 4.93. The T for these groups is -1.63 (df $= 682$, p $= .052$, one-tailed). The average group size did increase over the time period covered. It did not do so in a linear fashion, however. Nonetheless, the average group size was higher at the end of the period than at the beginning.

It was argued that group size would increase because a learning process would lead terrorists to commit more difficult acts as time progressed. It is, therefore, necessary to find out whether difficult acts were an increasing part of the terrorists' tactics during the period. Table 3.16 presents a percentage breakdown of difficult acts throughout the years 1968 to 1977.

The percentage of terrorist acts which can be classified as

TABLE 3.16

PERCENTAGE OF ALL TERRORIST ACTS CLASSIFIED AS DIFFICULT
BY YEAR

Year	N	Number of difficult acts	Percent difficult
1968	111	1	0.9
1969	166	3	1.8
1970	291	46	15.8
1971	244	26	10.7
1972	431	17	3.9
1973	286	49	17.1
1974	406	40	9.9
1975	327	56	17.1
1976	425	35	8.2
1977	308	33	10.7

TABLE 3.17

ONE-WAY ANOVA: GROUP SIZE BY REGION

Region	N	Mean Group Size
North America	81	2.36
Latin America	169	5.61
Western Europe	255	3.88
Eastern Europe	18	2.11
Africa	31	8.97
Middle East	141	4.07
Asia	73	4.48

grand mean=4.36   F=3.94   df=6, 761   p=.001   N=768

mean square:
    explained   234.78
    residual   59.63
    total   61.00

difficult fluctuates from year to year. It does seem to be somewhat higher on the average during the second half of the period. However, only 1968, 1969, and 1972 have very low percentages. It seems that if learning did take place, it took place
in the early years. The differences after 1969 are not very large,
except for the low percentage for 1972. The learning explanation offered for H1.9, therefore, is neither supported nor dis-
puted by Table 3.16.

HYPOTHESIS 1.10

Hypothesis H1.10 was tested by means of an ANOVA on
group size with region, as previously defined, independent.
H1.10 holds that the size of the acting group will vary from
region to region. The results of this test are shown in Table
3.17.

Table 3.17 does show that there is variation from region to
region in terms of the average size of the acting group. Africa

and Latin America have the highest averages, while Eastern Europe and North America have the smallest. In terms of policy, it would appear that authorities in Latin America and Africa must be prepared to deal with rather large groups of terrorists. Those in other regions must deal, usually, with smaller groups. In a direct contest with terrorists in Africa or Latin America, quite clearly, the authorities must be prepared to expend greater resources, especially manpower, if they are to be successful.

It may be that conditions in Latin America and Africa are such that terrorist organizations have an easier time recruiting and fielding large numbers of people than in other regions. This may be related to the living conditions in these regions, i.e., many authoritarian regimes and poverty. The size of the groups in Africa and Latin America may also be related to the number of terrorist groups associated with insurgencies in those regions. Insurgency movements would probably field a larger group because of their military or quasi-military structures. Moreover, the overall group size of insurgency movements may be larger, allowing them to put together a larger group. It is interesting to note that the other non-Western regions, except for Eastern Europe, also have larger than average mean acting groups, possibly for the same reasons. North America has a small mean acting group, although the reasons for this are not apparent.[1] Eastern Europe has the smallest mean group size, which may be an indication that Eastern European governments are efficient at preventing the recruitment of large numbers of terrorists who are opposed to the authorities in the region. Thus, while authoritarianism may lead to terrorist recruitment under most conditions, Eastern European governments may be more efficient at repressing terrorism than authoritarian regimes in Latin America and Africa. The results may also be partially due to incomplete reporting of terrorist events in Eastern Europe.

It would appear that regional variation in group size is partly a function of the types of action which occur in a region, given that most acts will be imitative rather than creative, and that many of the groups operating in a particular region have established a characteristic pattern of action.

TABLE 3.18

LARGE GROUP ACTS BY REGION

Region	N	N large group	% large group
North America	81	5	6.2
Latin America	169	32	18.9
Western Europe	255	27	10.6
Eastern Europe	18	1	2.3
Africa	31	7	22.6
Middle East	141	17	12.1
Asia	73	11	9.5
Total	768	100	13.0

In Table 3.18, data are presented on the number of acts within each region which can be classified as large group acts, i.e., those acts for which the acting group consisted of seven or more terrorists. This will provide better information on how prone a given region is to large group terrorist acts.

Table 3.18 shows that terrorist acts in Africa are the most likely to be committed by a large group, followed by Latin America and Asia. The other four regions are less likely to be the location of a large group act. Again, it appears that government policy in response to terrorist acts in Latin America and Africa must take into account the possibility that the terrorist group is large.

HYPOTHESIS 1.11

Hypothesis H1.11 holds, briefly, that acts committed by a terrorist coalition will tend to have a larger group size than will single group acts. This hypothesis was tested using a t-test. The result does not provide evidence for the hypothesis.

Single group acts had a mean of 4.89; coalitions had a mean of 5.10 (T = −.18, df = 549, p = .43, one-tailed). The average size of the coalitional group is larger, but only slightly so. The question remains, if coalitional acts generally consist of one group helping another commit an act which the former could not commit on its own, why is the average group size for coalitions not substantially larger than that for single group acts? The only reasonable response seems to be that there could be two variables determining the size of the coalitional act. The first is the actual groups involved; i.e., some groups simply prefer to act in smaller groups. Secondly, the perceived security risk which results from larger groups may prevent coalitions from forming a larger acting group than usual.[2]

A frequency count reveals that coalitions are slightly more likely to use a large acting group than are single groups. Only 15.6 percent of all single group acts were committed by a group of seven or more terrorists while 22.0 percent of all coalitional acts were committed by a large group. Coalitions are thus slightly more likely than single groups to use a large acting group.

At this point a brief listing of the findings related to group size can be offered.

- The average group size is largest for difficult acts.
- Difficult acts are more likely than other types of acts to be committed by a large group.
- There is some variance in group size from group to group, although most organizations use a relatively small group.
- Death is most likely to result from acts committed by intermediate-sized groups.
- Participants are most likely to be wounded during acts committed by intermediate-sized groups.
- Acts committed by intermediate-sized groups have the highest average number of deaths. Single actor events are second in terms of average deaths.
- Intermediate-sized group acts have the highest average number of wounded participants from terrorist acts.
- The average group size has become larger during the period under consideration.

- The average group size did not increase in a linear fashion.
- The largest average group sizes occur in Africa and Latin America while the smallest are in North America and Eastern Europe.
- Large group acts are most likely to occur in Africa and Latin America and least likely in Eastern Europe.

NOTES

1. In conversation with the author, Prof. Manfred Wenner has suggested one possible explanation for this finding. That is, in a highly industrialized nation it may take only a small number of terrorists to disrupt communications or transportation systems. A technologically dependent society is vulnerable to attack by small groups. One or two actors, for example, could deprive a large area of electrical power without much difficulty.

2. An alternative explanation is simply that most terrorist acts do not require a large group, and thus there is no reason for coalitional groups to use a larger strike force than there is for single groups to do so.

IV

HYPOTHESIS TESTING II: COALITIONS

HYPOTHESIS 2.1

The first proposition holds that a coalition will be less likely than a single group to be able to commit a complete terrorist act. A crosstabulation of completion status by whether a co-

TABLE 4.1

CROSSTABULATION OF COMPLETION STATUS BY PRESENCE OF COALITION

Status	Coalition Present?		
	No	Yes	Total
Incomplete	322 (17.5%) (93.9%)	21 (18.9%) (6.1%)	343 (17.5%)
Complete	1523 (82.5%) (94.4%)	90 (81.1%) (5.6%)	1613 (82.5%)
Total	1845 (94.3%)	111 (5.7%)	1956 (100%)

$Z1=-.424$ $\qquad$ $Z2=.424$

alition was present was performed to test the first hypothesis. The results of that test are shown in Table 4.1.

Table 4.1 does not support the hypothesis. The difference between the completion status of coalitional and single group acts is very small. There are two explanations which may explain this finding. First, it is possible that coalitions work out their command structures and assignments well enough in advance so that organizational problems do not arise during the act itself. Second, it seems plausible that if coalitions do usually consist of one group helping another to commit an act which the latter could not commit on its own, the additional resources brought to the act by another group may account for the high percentage of complete acts by coalitions. That is, the superior resources of coalitions make a complete act possible in spite of any organizational problems which may occur.

HYPOTHESIS 2.2

Hypothesis H2.2 holds that coalitions are less likely to be able to end a negotiated act in a peaceful manner, and thus there is a greater likelihood that deaths will result from a coalitional-negotiated act than from a single group act. Deaths resulted from 15.5 percent of all single group acts and 23.4 percent of all coalitional acts. It would appear that coalitions are slightly more prone to violent resolution of an act than are single groups. When only negotiated acts are included, single group acts result in deaths 12.1 percent of the time and coalitions result in deaths 30.0 percent of the time. Table 4.2 shows the results of a crosstabulation of whether deaths resulted by the presence of coalitions for negotiated acts.

Table 4.2 presents evidence which supports the hypothesis. Although the sample of coalitional-negotiated acts is small, they do appear to result in deaths far more often than do single group events by more than a two-to-one margin. Deaths result from 30 percent of all negotiated coalitional acts. The original belief, that coalitions will be less likely to reach internal agreement during bargaining, seems to be an adequate explanation. The Z-scores for Table 4.2 are highly significant, presenting additional evidence for H2.2.

TABLE 4.2

CROSSTABULATION OF RESULTING DEATH BY PRESENCE OF COALITIONS
FOR NEGOTIATED ACTS

Did Deaths Occur?	Coalition Present?		
	No	Yes	Total
No	450 (87.9%) (95.5%)	21 (70.0%) (4.5%)	471 (86.9%)
Yes	62 (12.1%) (87.3%)	9 (30.0%) (12.7%)	71 (13.1%)
Total	512 (94.5%)	30 (5.5%)	542 (100%)

$Z1 = 3.14**$ $Z2 = -3.14**$

*indicates $P < .10$ **indicates $P < .05$

HYPOTHESIS 2.3

Hypothesis H2.3 states that coalitional-negotiated acts will
have a higher average number of deaths than single group-
negotiated acts. Single group-negotiated acts averaged .68
deaths while coalitional-negotiated acts averaged 2.40 deaths
($T = -1.69$, $df = 540$, $p = .045$, one-tailed). The t-test supports
H2.3. The average number of deaths from coalitional-negotiated acts is nearly four times that for single group-negotiated
acts. This is consistent with expectations that coalitions will
tend to be more violent than single groups and that they will
be less able to reach internal agreement during bargaining.

There may also be additional reasons for this finding. It is
likely that coalitional acts end in a higher number of deaths
than single group acts for two reasons. First, they may have
greater resources, e.g., more powerful weapons, which allows
them to be more destructive. Second, it is possible that the
likelihood of deaths in single group and coalitional acts is equal,
but that once violence has started, a coalition still has a difficult time reaching internal agreement and thus the violence
does not end as quickly.

HYPOTHESIS 2.4

Hypothesis H2.4 is similar to H2.2. The fourth hypothesis on coalitions holds that participants are more likely to be wounded during negotiated coalitional acts than during single group-negotiated acts for the same reasons applied to H2.2 and H2.3. Overall, wounds resulted from 20.2 percent of the single group events and 25.2 percent of the coalitional acts. Wounds occurred during 16.1 percent of all single group-negotiated acts and 26.7 percent of all coalitional-negotiated acts. A crosstabulation for negotiated acts is presented in Table 4.3.

The evidence presented in Table 4.3 is moderately supportive of the hypothesis. The Z-scores are significant at less than .10. The frequencies show that participants are more likely to be wounded during coalitional acts than during single group acts. Participants were wounded in more than one quarter of all negotiated coalitional acts. The general tendency toward greater violence by coalitions is supported by the table.

TABLE 4.3

CROSSTABULATION OF RESULTING WOUNDS BY PRESENCE OF
COALITIONS FOR NEGOTIATED ACTS

Did Wounds Result?	Coalition Present?		
	No	Yes	Total
No	428	22	450
	(83.9%)	(73.3%)	(83.3%)
	(95.1%)	(4.9%)	
Yes	82	8	90
	(16.1%)	(26.7%)	(16.7%)
	(91.1%)	(8.9%)	
Total	510	30	540
	(94.4%)	(5.6%)	(100%)

$Z1 = 1.51*$ $Z2 = -1.51*$

*indicates P<.10   **indicates P<.05

HYPOTHESIS 2.5

The next hypothesis, H2.5, holds that the average number of wounded participants will be higher for negotiated coalitional acts than for single group acts. Coalitional acts averaged 2.67 wounded and single group acts averaged .95 (T = −1.83, df = 538, p = .034, one-tailed). Coalitional acts average more than twice as many wounded as do single group events. The t-test is significant at less than .05 (one-tailed). The evidence supports H2.5 strongly and provides further evidence that coalitions tend to be more violent than single groups.

HYPOTHESIS 2.6

Hypothesis H2.6 holds that negotiated coalitional acts are more likely than single group acts to result in property damage. When all acts are included, property damage results from 54.7 percent of all single group acts and 53.7 percent of all coalitional acts. There appears to be no difference overall. When

TABLE 4.4

CROSSTABULATION OF PROPERTY DAMAGE BY PRESENCE OF COALITION
DURING NEGOTIATED ACTS

Did Damage Occur?	Coalition Present?		
	No	Yes	Total
Yes	69 (15.0%) (95.8%)	3 (10.0%) (4.2%)	72 (14.7%)
No	390 (85.0%) (93.5%)	27 (90.0%) (6.5%)	417 (85.3%)
Total	459 (93.9%)	30 (6.1%)	489 (100%)

$Z1 = .746$ $Z2 = -.746$

only negotiated acts are included in the tally, property damage occurred during 15.0 percent of single group events and 10.0 percent of coalitional acts. The crosstabulation used to test H2.6 is shown in Table 4.4.

The table does not support the hypothesis. The result is much like that found for large groups. Indeed, single groups are more likely to commit acts which result in property damage, although the difference between the two categories is slight. An explanation for these findings, which are contrary to expectations, may be offered. It is possible that neither large groups nor coalitions are likely to engage in certain types of acts, i.e., bombings, which usually result in property damage. Therefore, when only negotiated acts are counted and bombings are absent, there appears to be no difference between the groups. It appears that coalitions are more violent when it comes to human casualties but no more likely to cause property damage.

HYPOTHESIS 2.7

Hypothesis H2.7 holds that coalitional acts as a percentage of all transnational terrorist acts should have increased during the period from 1968 to 1977. This hypothesis was tested by cross-tabulating coalitional acts by year. The results of that test appear in Table 4.5.

The table shows that there is a great deal of variance from year to year in terms of the frequency of coalitional acts. The chi-square value is high, indicating significant yearly variation. Nonetheless, the variation does not corroborate the general view among those who see terrorist cooperation as an increasing phenomenon. The table shows no linear increase in coalitional frequency. In 1972 coalitional activity increased dramatically and remained high through 1975, peaking in 1974. In 1976 and 1977 it fell back to pre-1972 levels. This is somewhat puzzling since there is significant variation, but not in the expected direction. It appears that coalitional acts were normally a very small portion of all terrorist acts; however, the period was marked by a four-year span of relatively high coalitional activity. One possible explanation for this is that

TABLE 4.5

CROSSTABULATION OF COALITIONAL ACTS BY YEAR OF OCCURRENCE

Coalition Present?			Year		
	68	69	70	71	72
No	78	95	177	136	250
	(98.7%)	(96.9%)	(95.2%)	(97.8%)	(93.6%)
	(4.1%)	(5.0%)	(9.4%)	(7.2%)	(13.3%)
Yes	1	3	9	3	17
	(1.3%)	(3.1%)	(4.8%)	(2.2%)	(6.4%)
	(.9%)	(2.7%)	(8.1%)	(2.7%)	(15.3%)
Total	79	98	186	139	267
	(4.0%)	(4.9%)	(9.3%)	(7.0%)	(13.4%)

Coalition Present?			Year			
	73	74	75	76	77	Total
No	208	245	215	249	231	1884
	(92.9%)	(89.1%)	(92.7%)	(96.9%)	(97.1%)	(94.4%)
	(11.0%)	(13.0%)	(11.4%)	(13.2%)	(12.3%)	
Yes	16	30	17	8	7	111
	(7.1%)	(10.9%)	(7.3%)	(3.1%)	(2.9%)	(5.6%)
	(14.4%)	(27.0%)	(15.3%)	(7.2%)	(6.3%)	
Total	224	275	232	257	238	1995
	(11.2%)	(13.8%)	(11.6%)	(12.9%)	(11.9%)	(100%)

chi-square=30.97   df=9   p=.001

coalitional activity may be infrequent during most years, i.e., under 4 percent of all acts, but may increase greatly for short periods of time as a result of specific terrorist campaigns conducted jointly by two or more groups with similar goals.

The explanation offered above is given strong support when yearly coalitional activities of specific groups are taken into account. The same two groups act together infrequently in most years, i.e., generally one or two acts. In 1972, however, the Comite Argentino de Lucha Anti-Imperialisto and the Ejercito Revolutionario del Pueblo committed five acts of transnational terrorism together. The next year, 1973, three acts were committed by Al-Fatah and the Popular Front for the Liberation of Palestine. In 1974, the peak year for coalitional activity, LAOS People Number One and LAOS Number Thirteen acted together seven times; Bandera Roja (Red Flag) and the National Liberation Armed Forces committed four acts together; the Popular Front for the Liberation of Palestine and the Commando Muhammed Boudia committed four coalitional acts; and the Cuban Youth Group acted together with El Condor three times. These four coalitional campaigns accounted for 18 of the 30 acts that occurred during 1974. Seven of the 17 acts that occurred during 1975 also involved El Condor and the Cuban Youth Group. The Popular Front for the Liberation of Palestine (a Middle Eastern group) and the Baader-Meinhof Gruppe (a West German group) acted together three times during 1975.

The evidence indicates that during the period from 1968 to 1977, coalitional activity did not increase in a linear fashion. Coalitional activity became more frequent in 1972 and remained high through 1975. Overall, coalitions account for only 5.6 percent of all terrorist acts. Coalitional activity is thus a small part of all terrorist activity. However, certain periods may see a major increase in coalitional activity due to one or more joint terrorist campaigns. Data for later periods could show a different trend; however, the evidence thus far does not support the belief that terrorist cooperation is becoming a large part of terrorist activity, i.e., the "terror network" is less cohesive than is often supposed. It does not preclude, however, the future possibility of one or several worldwide groups or partnerships. The policy implications of this are discussed in the next chapter.

HYPOTHESIS 2.8

Hypothesis H2.8 holds that coalitional acts are more likely than are single group acts to be difficult terrorist acts, or at least not simple acts. This is expected since terrorist coalitions are generally made up of one group helping another to commit an act which it could not commit on its own. A cross-tabulation of act difficulty by coalitions was done in order to test H2.8. The results are presented in Table 4.6.

TABLE 4.6

CROSSTABULATION OF DIFFICULTY OF THE TERRORIST ACT BY
PRESENCE OF TERRORIST COALITION

Difficulty	Coalition Present?		
	No	Yes	Total
Simple	1319	65	1384
	(75.1%)	(60.1%)	(74.3%)
	(95.3%)	(4.7%)	
Moderately	190	24	214
Difficult	(10.8%)	(22.4%)	(11.5%)
	(88.8%)	(11.2%)	
Difficult	247	18	265
	(14.1%)	(16.8%)	(14.2%)
	(93.2%)	(6.8%)	
Total	1756	107	1863
	(94.3%)	(5.7%)	(100%)

Z1=37.50**   Z2=38.67**   Z3=-9.00**

*indicates P<.10   **indicates P<.05

The data show that there are highly significant differences between single groups and coalitions in terms of the type of act committed. The Z-scores are, obviously, highly significant for all three types of acts.

Table 4.6 indicates that coalitions are only slightly more likely than single groups to commit difficult acts. However, they are much more likely to commit moderately difficult acts and much less likely to commit simple acts. While 75.1 percent of all single group acts were simple acts, only 60.1 percent of coalitional acts were simple. Simple acts still predominate in transnational terrorism and difficult acts are still comparatively rare. Nonetheless, it does appear that coalitions may in fact allow groups to commit acts which they could not commit on their own. For example, taken together, only 24.9 percent of single group events are difficult or moderately difficult and 39.2 percent of coalitional acts fall into one of these two categories. Coalitional acts are more than one and one-half times more likely to be difficult or moderately difficult than are single group acts. Of course, the evidence does not demonstrate conclusively that the individual groups involved in a coalition could not commit the specific act by themselves, but it does point strongly in that direction. Moreover, it is the best evidence available since information on the resources and capabilities of individual terrorist groups is difficult to collect.

HYPOTHESIS 2.9

The next hypothesis, H2.9, states that the frequency of coalitional activity will vary from one region of the world to another. A crosstabulation of coalitional activity by region is shown in Table 4.7.

The table illustrates that there is some variation in terms of frequency of coalitions from one region to another. Eastern Europe had no coalitions, although there were only 18 cases for that region, making any conclusion dubious if not impossible. Coalitions were comparatively rare in Asia and Africa. Western Europe had a slightly lower relative frequency of coalitional activity. North America, Latin America, and the Middle East had roughly the same relative frequency of coalitions. The crosstabulation does not show as much variation as was expected and this is reflected in the insignificant chi-square value for the table. It may be that there are many groups with similar goals in North America, Latin America, Western Europe, and the Middle East. Fewer coincidences of interest may occur in Africa and Asia. This would account for the variance that has been found. It would be difficult, however, to systematically demonstrate similarity of interest among the world's terrorist groups in order to support this explanation. In fact, since few groups have been thoroughly studied, it is not possible to do so.[1]

The evidence does indicate some regional variation in terms of coalitional activity. No single region, however, stands out as being the major center of terrorist cooperation. Rather, coalitions seem to be phenomena which occur in nearly every part of the world. They are still the exception and not the rule in transnational terrorism.

TABLE 4.7

CROSSTABULATION OF COALITIONAL ACTIVITY BY REGION

Coalition Present?	Region		
	North America	Latin America	Western Europe
No	289 (93.2%) (15.4%)	387 (93.7%) (20.6%)	690 (94.7%) (36.7%)
Yes	21 (6.8%) (8.9%)	26 (6.3%) (23.4%)	39 (5.3%) (35.1%)
Total	310 (15.6%)	413 (20.7%)	729 (36.6%)
	Eastern Europe	Africa	Middle East
No	18 (100%) (1%)	62 (98.4%) (3.3%)	297 (93.4%) (15.8%)
Yes	0 (0%) (0%)	1 (1.6%) (.9%)	21 (6.6%) (18.9%)
Total	18 (0.9%)	63 (3.2%)	318 (16.0%)
	Asia	Total	
No	137 (97.9%) (7.3%)	1880 (94.4%)	
Yes	3 (2.1%) (2.7%)	111 (5.6%)	
Total	140 (7.0%)	1991 (100%)	

chi-square=8.06   df=6   p=.234

HYPOTHESIS 2.10

Hypothesis H2.10 holds that terrorist coalitions, being basically alliances for offensive purposes, will usually be of short duration. The testing of this hypothesis is an intuitive process

TABLE 4.8

DURATION OF TERRORIST COALITIONS

Frequency	Coalitions	Percent	Cumulative Percent	Cumulative Number
7	2	2.9	2.9	2
6	1	1.5	4.4	3
5	1	1.5	5.9	4
4	3	4.4	10.3	7
3	2	2.9	13.2	9
2	9	13.2	26.4	18
1	50	73.5	100.0	68
Total	68	99.9		

based on frequencies of activity for specific coalitions. Overall, during the period covered by the data, 68 coalitions committed 111 transnational terrorist acts. In Table 4.8 data are presented showing the frequencies of attack for these 68 coalitions.

Table 4.8 provides strong evidence for the hypothesis. By far the majority of coalitions acted together only once, indicating that most terrorist coalitions were transitory. Indeed, the probability of a coalition acting two times or more is only .264. There is only a .132 chance that a coalition would be together through three acts, a .103 chance of it lasting for four or more acts, a .059 chance of a coalition lasting five or more acts, only a .044 chance of it lasting through six acts, and only a .029 chance that it would last through seven acts. Thus, nearly three-fourths of all coalitions committed only a single act of transnational terrorism. Less than 6 percent of all coalitions lasted through five or more acts. Table 4.8 offers evidence in support of H2.10. Terrorist coalitions are generally short-lived. Moreover, since coalitional acts made up less than 6 percent of all transnational terrorist acts, the evidence that a "terror network" or "terrorist international" exists is slight. If one does exist, it must have come into existence since 1977.

HYPOTHESIS 2.11

Even though Table 4.8 tends to confirm H2.10, it also offers evidence for H2.11, that some groups will form working partnerships, i.e., form a coalition which lasts through four or more acts. Few such partnerships existed during the 1968–1977 period. Only 10.3 percent of all coalitions were working partnerships. These seven partnerships accounted for 37 transnational terrorist acts, nearly a third of all coalitional acts. Thus, while working partnerships were not numerous, they did account for a large portion of all coalitional activity. Table 4.9 lists the seven working partnerships for the period from 1968 through 1977.[2]

Table 4.9 shows that there were some working partnerships formed during the 1968–1977 period. The most cooperative groups appear to be Al-Fatah and the Popular Front for the

TABLE 4.9 (a)

TRANSNATIONAL TERRORIST WORKING PARTNERSHIPS: 1968-1977

Coalition	Frequency	Percent of Coalitions
EC/CYG	7	6.3
L1/L13	7	6.3
BSO/AF	6	5.4
ERP/CALAI	5	4.5
BRRF/NLAF	4	3.6
PFLP/AF	4	3.6
PFLP/CMB	4	3.6
Total	37	33.3

[a] Because of space limitations it is not possible to list groups' full names involved in Tables 4.9 and 4.10. In order to aid the reader, each group's full name and abbreviation is as follows: PFLP = Popular Front for the Liberation of Palestine; AF = Al-Fatah; ERP = Ejercito Revolutionario del Pueblo; EC = El Condor; BSO = Black September Organization; L13 = Laos Number Thirteen; L1 = Laos People Number One; CYG = Cuban Youth Group; CALAI = Comite Argentino de Lucha Anti-Imperialisto; CMB = Commando Muhammed Boudia; PFLP–GC = Popular Front for the Liberation of Palestine-General Command; BRRF = Bandera Roja, Red Flag; NLAF = National Liberation Armed Forces.

Liberation of Palestine. Each of these two groups was involved in two working partnerships, one with each other. Altogether, 14 acts by working partnerships were carried out by coalitions of Palestinian groups. Close working relationships are apparently more frequent among Palestinian groups. This tends to indicate that working partnerships are a regional phenomenon and that coincidence of interest plays a major role in coalition formation. The leading coalitions, those with seven joint attacks, were among Asian and Latin American groups. Coalitional activity seems to be distributed among several regions, as noted above, in fairly equal measure. It is not the case that the Middle East is the most given to coalitional activity. However, it does seem to be the location of the most working partnerships. This is probably because these groups have similar goals, e.g., a Palestinian homeland, as opposed to groups in other regions whose motivations may be more diverse.

Since Al-Fatah and the Popular Front for the Liberation of Palestine each participated in working partnerships, an interesting question arises: Are some terrorist groups more likely than others to participate in coalitional acts? Are there certain groups that are just more cooperative than others? Given that some previous authors have argued that the Popular Front for the Liberation of Palestine has aided many groups in various ways, it is to be expected that it would participate in the most coalitional acts. This is exactly what the data show. The Popular Front for the Liberation of Palestine was involved in 26 coalitional acts, while Al-Fatah, in second place, was involved in only 13. Table 4.10 shows those transnational terrorist groups that were involved in five or more coalitional acts during the period covered by this study.

The Popular Front for the Liberation of Palestine has indeed been the most cooperative terrorist organization. Their 26 coalitional acts far outdistance all other groups. Moreover, they were involved in 23.4 percent of all coalitional acts. One organization was thus partly responsible for almost a quarter of all coalitional acts. Sixteen different groups, some from outside the Middle East, participated in coalitional acts with the Popular Front for the Liberation of Palestine. If a truly "international" terrorist group exists, the PFLP is it. Indeed, the

TABLE 4.10

FREQUENT PARTICIPANTS IN COALITIONAL ACTIVITIES

Group	Number of Acts	Percent of All Coalitional Acts
PFLP	26	23.4
AF	13	11.7
ERP	10	9.0
EC	10	9.0
BSO	9	8.1
L13	7	6.3
L1	7	6.3
CYG	7	6.3
CALAI	5	4.5
CMB	5	4.5
PFLP-GC	5	4.5

PFLP is the leading cooperative terrorist group. Al-Fatah, which was involved in 13 coalitional acts, was the second most cooperative group. El Condor and the Ejercito Revolucionario del Pueblo tied for third place in the rankings, but even that level of activity seems low in comparison to the PFLP.

The evidence indicates that most coalitions are of short duration, the vast majority lasting for only a single act. There were, however, some working partnerships formed during the 1968–1977 period. These partnerships have been identified. It has also been shown that some groups seem to be more cooperative than others. Specifically, the PFLP has participated in many coalitional acts with many different groups.

A brief summary of the findings related to terrorist coalitions is presented below.

· Deaths are more likely to result from coalitional acts than from single group acts.

- Participants are more likely to be wounded during coalitional acts than during single group acts.
- The average numbers of deaths and injuries are higher for coalitions than for single groups.
- Coalitional activity varies in frequency from year to year.
- Coalitional activity was highest from 1972 through 1975.
- Coalitions are more likely to engage in difficult acts of terrorism than are single groups.
- Eastern Europe, Africa, and Asia have little coalitional activity.
- North America, Latin America, Western Europe, and the Middle East have significant coalitional activity.
- Coalitions are relatively rare and account for only 5.6 percent of all terrorist acts.
- Coalitions usually do not last very long. Nearly three-fourths of all coalitions disband after only one act.
- There have been some terrorist organizations which formed working partnerships.
- Some groups were more likely than others to engage in coalitional activity.

NOTES

1. The assertion that this explanation cannot be demonstrated would be challenged by some writers on terrorism who claim to have systematically studied certain groups. Such studies usually present anecdotal evidence. Moreover, one cannot accept the alleged existence of a "terrorist international" or claims that all terrorism is directed by the Soviet Union as proof of coincidental interests among terrorist groups. There is no doubt that some groups have similar goals; however, no systematic study of the subject has been done. Therefore, the extent of coincidental interests is unknown.

2. A note of caution is necessary here. Since the data only covers the period from 1968 through 1977, it should not be assumed that the groups listed as being involved in coalitions during that period have behaved in the same way since that time. Without data after 1977, it is impossible to determine what coalitions currently exist.

V

COALITIONS, GROUP SIZE, AND POLICY

While this study is mainly concerned with increasing the level of understanding of terrorism and thereby advancing the discipline of political science, it nonetheless has relevance for decision makers as well. George (1980: 240) points out, for example, that social science theories may be relevant for policy making if they have diagnostic value, i.e., are able to increase a policymaker's understanding of a particular situation. Social science theories may also be helpful in predicting the consequences of alternative courses of action. Thus, this study is intended to have policy implications as well as extending the political organization approach to the study of transnational terrorism.

The necessity of policy-relevant research on terrorism is shown clearly by the fact that terrorism does not, at this writing, appear to be a decreasing phenomenon. It seems, rather, to be the method of choice for a variety of groups. Shribman (1984: 16E) reports 2,838 incidents of terrorism in 1983.[1] There were 10,159 deaths as a result of these actions during the year. The United States was involved in 77 incidents which resulted in 301 deaths.

The high frequency of terrorist acts, transnational or otherwise, has prompted the Reagan administration to take a hard line on terrorism. The administration's new antiterrorism policy is reported to include the possibility of preventive and retaliatory strikes on terrorist bases and camps abroad (Shribman, 1984: 16E). The use of such tactics presents some interesting issues regarding the sovereignty of states. For example, does the principle of state sovereignty bar the United States from making raids into foreign territories for what are essentially police activities? It is possible that the administration is unconcerned about violating the sovereignty of states which it believes are harboring terrorists. Nonethelss, the principle of state sovereignty would appear to allow states to grant haven to whomever they wish, disagreements about ideology with other nations notwithstanding.

The new antiterrorism policy, as presented to Congress, includes four bills. There is provision for rewards of up to $500,000 for information on acts of terrorism (Taylor, 1984: 4). The plan also proposes fines and prison terms of up to ten years for persons who provide training or other assistance to nations or groups designated by the Secretary of State as being involved in terrorism (Taylor, 1984: 1). The plan is aimed at preventing aid to nations that support terrorism (Taylor, 1984: 4).

Clearly, the administration feels that such steps are necessary to stem the tide of terrorism. However, the new plan raises some problems for domestic law as well as international law and has not been greeted enthusiastically by all concerned. The American Civil Liberties Union (ACLU), for example, has expressed concern that the provisions against aid are broad enough to be applied to many innocent actions aimed at bettering the lives of the citizens of other states. The bills also state that the Secretary of State's designation of a state as being supportive of terrorism cannot be challenged or raised as a defense by those charged under the law. Such provision obviously limits the ability of a defendant to respond to the government's case. It appears that measures which are viewed by some as necessary to prevent terrorism are seen by others as an infringement on civil liberties, at least in democratic nations.

Popular or not, the new plan of the Reagan administration

demonstrates the concern of policymakers over the inability of the government to prevent terrorism, although there may be no real reason to expect more success against political terrorism than against other forms of criminal behavior which the government has also failed to prevent. The new policy may be partly the result of political forces. There may be a demand that something be done about what is, at this particular time, a visible threat to society.

Another sign of the perceived relevance of studies related to antiterrorism policy is the fact that risk consulting, an industry whose function is to prevent terrorist attacks on corporations, is a growing industry. Control Risks Ltd. and Ackerman and Palumbo, Inc., for example, each bring in more than $4,000,000 per year in revenues for advising clients on how to avoid terrorism. Control Risks Ltd. sells a constantly updated data base retrieval service which carries current information on the risks of doing business in 60 different countries. The industry is growing due to increasingly frequent terrorist attacks. Rand Corporation, for instance, estimates that the frequency of international terrorist attacks is increasing at a rate of 17 percent per year (Passow, 1984: 14F-15F).

Regardless of the forces behind the new policy, it is aimed at a phenomenon which shows no sign of abating. Therefore, policy-relevant studies of terrorism are needed to inform policymakers. Clearly, the better the information available to policymakers, the more likely a policy is to be successful.

GROUP SIZE AND TERRORISM POLICY

Group size may affect policy in several ways. At the operational level, group size is likely to influence the course of bargaining in negotiated terrorist acts. Intuitively, it is apparent that the larger the terrorist group, the more likely there is to be a variety of opinion within the group. Negotiation must take place between the terrorists and the authorities and within the terrorist group. Thus, an agreement will be more difficult to reach.

For policymakers this means that they should be cognizant of the possibility that, during large group events, they may not be dealing with a monolithic organization; i.e., there may be various opinions represented within the terrorist group. They must take account of the possibility that negotiation may fail because of internal disagreements within the terrorist group. Large groups thus pose a more difficult negotiation problem than do small groups. Alternately, it is possible that a large group may have a command structure which allows for the control of the negotiation process without the input of individual members.

Hilton (n.d.) argues that in order to end an act of terrorism without suffering the destruction threatened by the terrorists, the authorities must give in to some part of the terrorists' demands, i.e., pay some risk premium. It seems logical that satisfying the required part of the demands of many actors, whose ideologies vary, will be more costly than satisfying the demands of a small number. Thus, the risk premium paid to end a large group act will likely be larger than that paid to end a small group act.

In terms of ending a negotiated act without violence, however, intermediate groups, rather than large groups, seem to be the most violent. Almost 40 percent of all intermediate group negotiated acts end in violence. Why should it be the case that intermediate groups are more prone to violence than either large groups or small groups? The most likely reason for this is that intermediate groups are likely to combine the features of large and small groups.

Intermediate groups will have a wide range of internal opinions, much like large groups. They are also like small groups in that their actions may depend largely upon the personal idiosyncracies of a few leading members. An extremist is likely to exercise more control over an intermediate group than over a large group. The cost of satisfying both a variety of demands and extreme demands may be too high for the authorities to pay. Thus, a violent ending results.

This points out another facet of group size as it relates to negotiation. Small groups may be more influenced by extreme members than large groups, assuming that personal influence is proportionate to group size. It is possible that the violence which results from small group negotiated acts may be partly the result of the personal ideological orientation of extreme members.

It is clear that small, intermediate, and large group acts each pose their own set of distinctive requirements on authorities. Policymakers must be cognizant of these particular qualities when planning negotiation strategies.

Those acts which have been defined as difficult logistically are more likely to be committed by a large terrorist group than are other types of acts. Indeed, the mean group size for difficult acts in 7.74, compared with 4.11 for moderately difficult acts, and 4.40 for simple acts. From a policy perspective this means two things: it may be possible to estimate the size of the acting group given that a certain type of act has been committed, and even though the average group size overall is small, some types of acts have a characteristically larger group size. Knowing these findings can be an aid to policymakers in determining how to respond to a terrorist act. If it is an act which is associated with a large group, it may require a larger responding force. Being able to estimate, within a reasonable range, the number of terrorists involved has distinct advantages for the responding authority.

Such authority may, for example, set a policy that greater manpower will be diverted from other tasks to respond to certain terrorist acts. An appropriate response policy could also discourage an attempt to attack the terrorists if a large group is suspected, since a larger group would be harder to subdue than a smaller group and presents greater possibilities of casualties.

Policymakers also must account for overall organizational size when attempting to understand specific groups operating within a given jurisdiction. It seems, from the data presented, that large groups are capable of acts which small groups are not, and that large groups may have a greater choice of tactics than small groups. Terrorist organizations that are capable of fielding a large acting group have a larger choice of tactics than those who can gather only a small acting group. Moreover, knowing a group's characteristic acting force size may give clues as to its likely choice of tactics.

The size of the group varies from one organization to another. The data indicate that most groups normally operate with a small acting group, i.e., between about three and four members. Some groups may field much larger acting forces. The ERP acting group, for example, averaged 6.58 members. Groups whose characteristic acting force is larger than average may be able to commit more difficult acts of terrorism and may have a greater choice of tactics. Policymakers should consider these factors in deciding how to deal with specific groups and planning responses to specific acts.

Group size appears to have effects on the ability of a group to complete an act of terrorism once begun. Earlier, it was believed that internal differences of opinion and an increased security risk would make it more difficult for large groups to carry out complete acts of terrorism. However, it appears that large groups do not face any more difficulty than intermediate groups. Single actors, perhaps because they rely only on themselves and face a minimal security risk, are the most likely to commit a complete act. Small groups are the least able to do so. Why small groups should have such difficulties is a perplexing question. Possibly larger groups, i.e., intermediate and large groups, may be able to finish an act even if some members defect from the acting group. Small groups may be more dependent on the actions of individual members and have no margin of error.

A policymaker could well ask whether this finding is of any significance to decision making by the authorities. The major importance is that policymakers must be prepared to deal with complete acts of terrorism. Less than 20 percent of all acts are stopped before they are logistically complete. Small groups are somewhat less likely to complete an act than are other groups, although the difference is slight. Basically, it means that policymakers must be prepared to contend with acts presented as essentially complete. Only rarely has the logistical success of an act been prevented.

A question arises as to whether the responding authorities may be partly responsible for this condition. It may be that authorities have placed too many resources into the operational phase of response, i.e., responding to a complete act, and not enough into preincident planning. Preincident planning would include all elements designed to make the completion of a terrorist act more difficult. How the available resources are allocated to each phase is a decision for policymakers to make themselves.

There is little, if any, policy relevance to the findings relating to the size of the acting group over time. The group size does seem to be larger for the latter half of the period than for the first half. However, there is no linear upward trend in group size or in difficult acts of terrorism over the period covered by the data. This seems to give credence to those scholars who argue that terrorism is an imitative phenomenon.

Significant variation has been found across regions in terms of group size. Africa, with a mean of 8.97 persons, and Latin America, with a mean of 5.61, have the highest average group sizes. Policymakers whose area includes these two regions should be cognizant of the fact that they are likely to be dealing with larger than normal groups. Greater resources may be required to respond to some regions than to others. However, since most responses are still a matter of national action, this finding may have less significance than it would if there were an international organization charged with responding to transnational terrorism.

TERRORIST COALITIONS AND POLICY

There are several findings of relevance for policymakers in the study of coalitions presented here. For example, some authors claim that coalitions generally take the form of one group assisting another in the commission of an act which the first group could not carry out on its own. This view is given some credence by the results of the data analysis. It appears that coalitions are more likely than single groups to commit terrorist acts which qualify as difficult or moderately difficult. When two or more groups act together, their combined resources are, of course, greater than the resources of one group alone. This finding raises several issues for policymakers.

Policymakers should take note of the fact that coalitions can commit difficult acts of terrorism more easily than can single groups. Thus, it seems that coalitions have a wider choice of tactics than do single groups. Those responsible for planning policies to combat transnational terrorism should be aware that when two groups have formed a working partnership, they will be more likely to commit logistically difficult acts and will have a greater choice of tactics than the groups would have on their own.

Moreover, since they are able to bring greater resources to their task, coalitions are more likely than single groups to be innovative in terms of tactics. Terrorism is usually an imitative phenomenon. However, coalitions, if they so desire, seem to have a better chance to be creative. Coalitions have the talents, financial resources, and weapons that are needed to commit new types of acts. Only large and well-financed single groups could do so.

Coalitions also seem to be of great benefit to small, poorly financed and equipped groups. Such groups could commit only simple, hit-and-run type events on their own. If they form a coalition with a larger, well-financed group, their choice of tactics and their available resources will increase. They will be able to carry out acts they could not commit on their own. It is possible for small terrorist groups, over a period of time, to develop contacts and partnerships with a number of other groups and thus increase their power.

The data does not present information on which terrorist groups are giving aid to other groups, except at the operational level of the transnational terrorist act. It is likely, however, given the distribution of coalitional activity across groups, that some groups act as the major powers in a terrorist international subsystem. A few large groups could provide aid to other groups of similar ideological orientation. The larger and smaller groups stand in a patron-client relationship to each other. In this way terrorist groups may form political blocs, much as nation-states do. Unfortunately, reliable data on patron-client relationships, the financial condition of terrorist groups, their memberships, and other resources is difficult to obtain. Most of the information in the literature is based on estimates. Nonetheless, it is possible for transnational terrorist groups to form a number of "terrorist foreign policy subsystems." If this is in fact the case, transnational terrorist behavior may be much like that of nation-states.

From a policy perspective this means that there is no single "terrorist international." There may, however, be several regional or ideological networks, "blocs," of terrorist groups. It may be that terrorism could be more effectively combatted by taking account of the fact that entire blocs must be stopped, rather than concentrating efforts on single groups.

It is clear that the presence of a coalition affects the outcome of a negotiated terrorist act. It is expected that during a coalitional act, negotiation must take place within the terrorist acting group as well as between the acting group and the authorities. Moreover, it is more likley that there will not be internal agreement in the terrorist acting group if a coalition is present. This leads to a greater probability of a violent outcome rather than a peaceful, negotiated solution. The data show that deaths occurred in 30.0 percent of all coalitional-negotiated acts, but only 12.1 percent of all single group negotiated acts. The chances of deaths resulting are more than doubled by the presence of a coalition. Moreover, participants were wounded in 26.7 percent of coalitional-negotiated acts versus 16.1 percent of single group negotiated acts. Violent outcomes to negotiated terrorist acts are to be expected when a coalition is present.

Coalitional-negotiated acts also result in far more deaths on the average than do single group negotiated acts. This is due, in part, to the inability of coalitions to reach internal agreements. It may also be partly due to the greater resources of coalitions. A terrorist coalition may have greater firepower than a single group, and this may account for part of the variation.

To the policymaker who deals with transnational terrorism, these findings suggest a greater tendency toward violence on the part of terrorist coalitions. Policymakers must be prepared for longer periods of negotiation with coalitions. The "risk premium" which authorities must pay to a coalition will be higher than for a single group because they must satisfy the minimum utility requirements of two or more groups rather than one. Authorities must also be prepared for a violent outcome when a coalition is involved in a transnational terrorist act. Not only is there likely to be violence, it will probably be more severe than the violence resulting from a single group event.

The presence of a coalition apparently has nothing to do with whether the acting group is able to carry the transnational terrorist act to completion. The security problem supposed by some scholars to exist for coalitions does not seem to be a major influence on the ability of the acting coalition to carry out an act of terrorism.

A number of authors have suggested that coalitional activity is an increasing phenomenon, at least insofar as all transnational terrorist cooperation is increasing. If this were the case, policymakers would have to be prepared for more violent outcomes to terrorist events because coalitional acts are more likely than single group acts to end in violence. The data for the period from 1968 to 1977 do not support the belief that coalitional activity is increasing. For the period under consideration, coalitional activity was, for the most part, rare. However, there was one period, from 1972 through 1975, when coalitional activity increased substantially over previous levels. After this period, the level of coalitional activity returned to its pre-1972 level. There was no linear increase in coalitional activity during the period covered by the data. It is, of course, possible that it has increased since that time.

During the period covered by the data, few coalitional acts occurred during an average year. During those years when coalitional activity was high, the increase appears to have been the result of a small number of coalitions attacking repeatedly. A small number of joint terrorist campaigns accounted for most of the deviation from the usual pattern of little coalitional activity.

The policy relevance of regional variation in coalitional activity is slight. Eastern Europe, Africa, and Asia seem to have relative immunity to coalitional activity. North America, Latin America, Western Europe, and the Middle East are all subject to coalitional acts. There is very little variation among those four regions in terms of coalitional frequency. Still, coalitional acts are rare in comparison to single group events; coalitions do not account for more than 6.8 percent of all transnational terrorist acts in any region.

The data also show that coalitions are generally short-lived. Nearly three-quarters of all transnational terrorist coalitions lasted for only a single act. Only about one coalition in ten lasted through four or more acts, and none committed more than seven during the period under consideration. For policymakers it means that just because two or more groups have committed a coalitional act, there is no reason to assume that coalitional activity will become their normal manner of operation. Policymakers will rarely have to concern themselves with long-lasting coalitions.

Even though most coalitions are short-lived, transnational terrorist groups do sometimes form working partnerships. During the period covered by the data, seven working partnerships were formed. These seven alliances committed 37 coalitional acts of transnational terrorism. They were thus responsible for 33.3 percent of all coalitional acts. Therefore, 10.3 percent of all coalitions were responsible for one-third of all coalitional acts. Although they are comparatively rare, working partnerships commit a disproportionately large share of all coalitional acts.

Policymakers should also be alert to the finding that certain terrorist groups are more likely than others to be involved in coalitional activites. When policymakers suspect that a certain group is involved in an act, they may have reason to believe that a coalition is present and plan accordingly. Authorities may wish to plan for the possibility of a violent outcome and for difficult negotiations. They may also want to consider the coalitional activity level of a group in planning long-range strategies for dealing with that group.

Some groups appear to act as patrons to many other groups by committing coalitional acts with several partners. The PFLP, for example, carried out transnational terrorist coalitional acts with 16 other groups. Moreover, the PFLP was involved in nearly one-quarter of all coalitional acts during the period from 1968 through 1977. Coalitional activity seems to be part of the PFLP's normal operating procedure.

There remains a question of whether the future is likely to

see the development of a worldwide terrorist group or permanent coalition of groups. The PFLP appears to have come
closest to forming a worldwide network of groups. However,
there does not seem to be strong evidence that a single terrorist network has formed or will form. It is possible that several
groups could, through coalitional activity and effective use of
modern transportation systems, develop into worldwide groups
with the ability to strike nearly any target anywhere in the
world.

From a political perspective it seems more likely that several groups could develop the ability to act worldwide than that
a single "international terrorist network" will form with some
nation-state or large terrorist group at its head. Politically, it
would require a coincidence of interest among many terrorist
groups for a single worldwide network to be effective. Such
similarity of interests among a large enough number of groups
is unlikely to occur. Transnational terrorist groups, like other
political organizations, have a variety of goals and ideologies.
Terrorist organizations appear to be as issue-specific as other
political interest groups. Even where some area of agreement
may exist between two groups, there may be other issues on
which the groups differ. There may be occasional instances
where two or more groups can agree to terms for the commission of a single act. There may be enough similarity of interests among several groups for a large-scale working partnership to be formed. However, it seems very unlikely that a single
terrorist network could be formed which would dominate
worldwide terrorist activity.

TERRORISM, INTERNATIONAL LAW, AND
THE UN

One aspect of national and international policy towards terrorism is how it is to be treated by international organizations
and international law. While this study is not primarily concerned with international law, there are several aspects of law
and organization which must be considered in light of transnational terrorism.

The major observation which can be made at this point about

international organizations, especially the United Nations, and terrorism policy is that the pluralistic nature of international organizations makes agreement on policy difficult. The UN has had difficulty in dealing with terrorism because, for ideological reasons, the organization cannot agree on a definition of terrorism. When in 1972 the UN did undertake a study of terrorism, its report focused on the alleged causes, rather than the control, of terrorism (Wardlaw, 1982: 105-106). The UN has, however, passed conventions against violence aimed at internationally protected persons (1973) and the taking of hostages (1979). The 1979 convention received little attention from member states, but the 1973 accord has been ratified by 49 states (Wardlaw, 1982: 110-112). Friedlander (1979, Vol. 1: 47) argues that the UN even views terrorism as an acceptable practice provided it is associated with a "national liberation movement." Yoder (1983b: 510) echoes this view. He points out that while the UN has passed a resolution against terrorism, a general convention is unlikely to win approval. This situation results in part from the fact that the Third World does not want to take a stand against "movements against colonial, racist, and alien regimes," and is partly due to the unwillingness of the Soviet Union to oppose "revolutionary movements."

Yoder (1983a: 588) argues that even though they are marred by the difficulties just discussed, UN resolutions do increase international cooperation against terrorism. In contrast to resolutions, conventions give more enforcement power. However, so far only aircraft, nuclear terrorism, hostages, and diplomatic personnel are covered by conventions. Thus, there is a large weakness in that many terrorist events are not covered by conventions.

Several other authors have treated the role of the UN in combatting transnational terrorism. Shamwell (1983) focuses on the implementation of the convention on crimes against diplomatic and internationally protected persons. McDonald (1983) discusses the events leading to passage of the UN convention on hostage taking. Finger (1976) provides an excellent general review of UN activities on terrorism.

It seems that the pluralistic nature of the UN prevents it

from taking real action against terrorism. Indeed, its members may be more concerned with determining the justice of a particular cause espoused by certain terrorist groups than with the protection of victims. The wide variety of membership and ideology makes a cohesive policy unlikely.

The International Civil Aviation Organization (ICAO) is one international organization that has had success in its battle against terrorism and airplane hijacking. In recent decades a threat to the safety of airline travel has developed. The ICAO has been largely successful in at least slowing down the threat. For example, there were 245 airplane hijackings in the 1969–1971 period, but only 147 in the 1978–1980 period (Finger, 1983: 520).

The success of the ICAO has come largely as the result of its three major conventions. The first convention was the 1963 Tokyo Convention. This was followed by the Hague Convention in 1970 and the Montreal Convention in 1971 (Finger, 1983: 520).

The ICAO conventions provide for harsh treatment of hijackers. The Hague Convention, for example, requires that offenders be prosecuted or extradited and that hijacking be punished by "severe penalties." The Montreal Convention has similar provisions which deal with offenses committed while an aircraft is on the ground (Finger, 1983: 521-522).

The ICAO has also been able to get a large number of nations to accept the conventions. There were 110 states which had ratified the Tokyo Convention, 114 for the Hague Convention, and 113 for the Montreal Convention by June of 1982 (Finger, 1983: 522). In addition to the three major conventions, the ICAO has also taken an active role in developing security programs for nations to use in the prevention of hijacking (Finger, 1983: 525).

Another question is how terrorism is to be viewed in international law, especially the generally accepted, though not always followed, rules of war. One of the earliest attempts to codify rules for war was the Just War Doctrine which held, among other principles, that a war must be waged by a competent authority (government) in defense of a state (Fenwick, 1965: 57). Essentially, legitimate war had to be waged by a state. A state had to possess territory and sovereignty, i.e., could not be subject to a higher authority (Fenwick, 1965: 125). Levi (1976: 39) declares that a state is sovereign when "there is no higher authority directing its behavior, when it is free to make its own political decisions."

Under traditionally understood international law, war is to be waged by a sovereign state. Transnational terrorists generally are not held to possess sovereignty and usually do not have legal jurisdiction over any territory. But the question is, do all recognized states possess sovereignty? Certainly some states have more control over their own actions than others, and terrorists may possess freedom from higher authority in fact if not in law. According to international law all states are equal and sovereign. This is a legal condition which does not necessarily match reality. It is obvious that some recognized states are not truly sovereign and even more obvious that not all states are equal.

In Chapter 2 it was shown that transnational terrorists are significant actors in the international system and that they possess autonomy. Here, it has been suggested, not all states are as free from other authority as the law argues and that many transnational terrorist organizations are as "sovereign" as many states. Therefore, it is possible to view transnational terrorism as a form of warfare in the international legal system. But what does this mean for the "rules of war"?

Fenwick (1965: 654-656) lists the general principles of warfare. Among the most important are:

- The force used should be in proportion to the end which war is supposed to serve.
- Force should not exceed what is necessary.
- Force should have no object except the submission of the enemy.
- Violence should not be inhumane.
- Noncombatants should not be attacked.

Whether transnational terrorism does or can meet the first four requirements is open to debate. It depends largely on how one defines humane and necessary. The last requirement, however, is violated repeatedly by transnational terrorists.

Terrorists do not usually attack soldiers, let alone soldiers who are in a legal state of war with them. Indeed, terrorists attack persons who are often not involved at all in their disputes with whatever authority they are attempting to influence.

Even if transnational terrorism is held to constitute warfare, legitimate or not, the chances for international legal control of terrorism do not appear to be good. It is doubtful that the world's nations could agree on any form of legal control of terrorism, given that they cannot agree on a definition. It is also unlikely that transnational terrorists would submit to any form of international legal control, and under current circumstances, adherence to international law is often a voluntary matter. Realistically, acts of terrorism are violations of criminal laws in most nations and this has not prevented them. It is improbable that international law would fare much better.

Yet another international legal problem is posed by the possibility of some states granting haven to terrorists whose extradition is requested by another state. Ideological sympathy, for example, could lead a regime to refuse extradition. Under international law there is virtually no way that one state can force another to extradite a terrorist. Fenwick (1965: 394) points out that even in treaties of extradition political offenses are excluded from the requirement that an offender be extradited. Thus, a state presumably can grant haven to a terrorist simply by declaring the offense to be political. Here the sovereignty of the individual state works against the efficient enforcement of criminal justice.

Yet another problem is posed by international or interstate terrorism. A state that sponsors or conducts terrorism against another state poses a problem for its victim states. Since they are legally recognized states, states conducting terrorist campaigns do have a legal right to make war. However, like transnational terrorists, they are usually in violation of the prohibition against attacks on noncombatants. Nonetheless, the legal remedies available may not be viable. Assuming that a victimized state could get the UN to condemn another state for terrorist acts, of what practical value would the declaration be? The UN would not be likely to take substantive action against the terrorist state. Thus, the only practical remedy would be to use the national forces of the victimized state to punish the offender. The enforcement of the law would still be a national matter.[2]

GENERAL POLICY CONSIDERATIONS

Two general considerations are of relevance to policymakers. The first is the enduring nature of transnational terrorism. Policymakers have attempted to deal with the phenomenon of transnational terrorism for more than a decade. As of this writing, transnational terrorism shows no signs of declining. Since data are not presently available, it is impossible to say whether it is increasing. However, current events would suggest that it has not decreased. Transnational terrorism, therefore, is likely to continue to occupy policymakers for the near future. Obviously, a response adequate to end transnational terrorism has not taken place. This brings about the second general consideration.

For transnational terrorism to be stopped would require the cooperation of the proper authorities in virtually every nation. Terrorist coalitions may be difficult to organize, but antiterrorist coalitions are nearly impossible. It is unlikely that any international coalition against terrorism will be formed. Logistically, it would be difficult to coordinate a worldwide response. The major drawback, however, is that the world's nations have so far had a difficult time even agreeing that terrorism is a problem. They cannot agree on a definition of terrorism. The evidence collected so far indicates that some states actually support certain terrorist groups. Such nations would be obviously opposed to an international organization designed to end terrorism. Many nations seem to take an ideological view of terrorism: those they agree with are not terrorists, while those they disagree with are, regardless of whether either group actually commits acts of terrorism. In short, no international response can be expected. It may, however, be possible for some nation-states within a particular region or having a particular ideological orientation in common to form antiterrorist coalitions without regard to the existing structure of international organizations.

This chapter has presented several findings which are relevant to decision makers whose responsibilities include formulating policies on transnational terrorism. Most of these findings have importance at the operational level. However, they may also affect long-range policy making in that they may be considered in establishing overall policies for response to transnational terrorist acts. These policy-relevant findings and suggestions as to how they may affect policy are not intended as specific recommendations to policymakers. Government responses to transnational terrorism must be developed by those who have official responsibility for dealing with the phenomenon. The findings presented here and the policy relevance discussed should not be taken as evidence for or against specific policies.

NOTES

1. The unusually high number may come about from the method of counting by Risks International, which gathered the data. It is not clear whether this represents transnational, international, domestic, or all types of terrorism. Nor is there a definition of terrorism provided which would clarify these matters.

2. Israel, for example, presented an interesting example of national enforcement when it invaded the territory of neighboring Lebanon in order to drive out the PLO which it claimed was launching terrorist attacks against Israel from Lebanese territory. It was not a case of interstate terrorism. Nonetheless, Israel claimed that Lebanon had failed to control the PLO and that, therefore, Israel would take the task on itself. Such an invasion may be an extreme case of national means of enforcement, but it does show that a nation may feel obligated to take extreme measures against what it believes to be terrorist attacks sanctioned by another government.

VI

CONCLUSION

FINDINGS ON GROUP SIZE

In this study, group size has been shown to be a key variable operationally in several ways. At this point, the major findings should be restated. Those findings are:

- Difficult acts have the largest average group size.
- Difficult acts are more likely to be committed by a large group than are simple or moderately difficult acts.
- There is some variance in average group size from group to group, although the significance of this variance is not known. In the future, a sufficient number of groups may have established a characteristic pattern of behavior so that we will be able to determine what characteristics of the groups are responsible for the variation.
- Intermediate-sized groups are the most likely to commit transnational terrorist acts which result in death for one or more participants.
- Intermediate-sized groups are the most likely to commit transnational terrorist acts which result in one or more participants being wounded.
- The average number of deaths resulting from negotiated transnational terrorist acts is greatest for intermediate groups, followed by single individuals.

· The average number of persons wounded is highest for intermediate groups involved in negotiated acts of terrorism.

· The average size of the terrorist groups changed during the period under consideration. It is higher for the second half of the period than for the first. However, this change does not appear to be in response to a change in tactics during the period.

· The average group size did not increase in a linear fashion during the period covered by the data.

· Africa and Latin America are the regions with the largest average group sizes, while North America and Eastern Europe have the smallest averages.

· Large group acts of terrorism are most likely to occur in Africa and Latin America, and least likely in Eastern Europe.

These findings present several issues for social science research efforts aimed at understanding the phenomenon of transnational terrorism. This study has offered some suggestions, for example, as to how the size of the acting group affects the process of bargaining between terrorists and authorities and within the terrorist group itself. It would, of course, be preferable to have direct evidence on the internal bargaining processes of transnational terrorist groups. So far, social scientists have managed to gather only very limited information on the internal decision-making processes of terrorist groups. Although the decision structures of terrorist groups are not likely to be made public by the groups themselves, social scientists may be able to approximate those structures in order to develop a better understanding of terrorist decision making.

It is probably not possible, in the short term, for social scientists to develop a comprehensive understanding of the overall decision-making systems used by terrorist organizations. However, they may be able to find out how terrorists bargain internally during the course of a terrorist act through the use of simulations. Transnational terrorist acts could be simulated following Sloan's (1981) work on the subject. The simulations could be carried out using "terrorist groups"of various sizes. No internal bargaining rules could be specified. However, various combinations of ideological diversity and cohesion could be tested in order to separate the effects of ideological diversity from the effects of group size. Such simulations may allow social scientists to see how decisions are made within acting terrorist groups, and allow for the testing of the effects of group size and ideological cohesion as well. Among the issues to be investigated should be: Are large terrorist groups less able to reach internal agreement than small groups? And is the behavior of small groups determined more by individual personalities than that of large groups?[1]

Exchange theories of interest group behavior (Olson, 1971; Moe, 1980; Frohlich, Oppenheimer, and Young, 1971) tend to suggest that the internal life of a political organization may include significant ideological differences. That is, the views of the members toward various purposive goals of the group may have considerable variance. Indeed, an actor could join a group whose purposive goals he opposes, or is indifferent to, simply because the benefits he derives from the selective incentives of the group are large enough to justify the cost of his participation. It is interesting to note that few efforts have been made to study empirically the internal cohesion of interest groups. Olson's (1971) work, and Frohlich, Oppenheimer, and Young's (1971), were produced without data. They are completely deductive. Moe's (1980) work has little data, and nothing directly on cohesion. Thus, the degree of internal cohesion among even normal interest groups remains open to dispute. Nonetheless, social scientists could enhance their understanding of transnational terrorism if evidence of the degree to which particular terrorist groups were ideologically cohesive were available. Intuitively, it seems that the greater the selective incentives a group offers, the larger its membership. And the larger its membership, the more likely there is to be ideological diversity within the group.

Few previous studies have considered the effects of group size on transnational terrorism. Virtually nothing has been written about its operational effects on the terrorist act. Indeed, even those studies that have considered the overall size of a terrorist organization (Wilkinson, 1979b; Wolf, 1978a; Mickolus, 1981; Gurr, 1979; Grabosky, 1979) have given almost no attention to how size interacts with the decision-making structure of the group or how it affects the ideological cohesion. Moreover, they have paid no attention to the role of factors aside from ideology which may be used to attract and maintain an organization's membership.

Our understanding of transnational terrorism also requires a greater interest in how terrorists operate. That is, what tactics do they use? Specifically, further work is needed to determine just how the ability of the terrorist organization to field or not field a large acting group influences its choice of tactics. It seems reasonable to assume that an organization capable of putting together a large group has a greater choice of tactics than do other groups. Social scientists may also wish to investigate the role of selective incentives in enabling terrorist organizations to utilize a large acting group. In this investigation the resources and funding of transnational terrorist groups is crucial since financial resources are needed in order to provide selective incentives.

Comparative work should also be done on the characteristic size of the acting groups used by different organizations. What variables seem to influence this characteristic of a specific group? Is it related to funding levels? Selective incentives? Overall size of the group?

The present study has shown that the size of the acting group has no effect on the ability of the group to complete an act of terrorism. This finding is somewhat puzzling in that it is counterintuitive. However, for the time being it will have to remain an unexplained finding.

The findings of this study as they relate to the peacefulness or violence of particular outcomes for negotiated terrorist acts are also different than those which were initially expected. Deaths or injuries are most likely to occur during intermediate group acts. Large groups are not, therefore, the most likely to commit an act which ends violently. The question is, however, why are intermediate groups so likely to commit acts which end in violence?

This work has suggested that this finding results from the expectation that intermediate-sized transnational terrorist groups will combine the lack of internal cohesion of larger groups with the personality influences of small groups. Such a combination of factors might account for this finding. It is also a subject for further investigation. It relates, again, to the size of the group affecting the decision-making process of the acting group. The likelihood of a violent outcome for any act of a specific size can be studied using terrorist simulations. In this way the relative influences of personality and ideological diversity may become apparent. Obviously, simulations are not the ideal way of investigating the internal structure of a transnational terrorist group. However, unless the terrorists themselves are willing to provide the information, it may be the best available method for use by social scientists.

This study also found that single actor events result in a large number of deaths. They are a close second to intermediate group events. The best explanation for this may be ideology: a person who carries out an act of terrorism alone is likely to be very committed ideologically and unwilling to compromise with authorities. These individuals may also be able to justify killing because of their ideologies. Of course, more work is needed before this explanation can be supported or shown to be untrue.[2]

The findings related to regional and temporal variation in group size are not as interesting theoretically as the other findings. They may be the result of many things, such as specific groups being active at a given time or in a particular region. However, if later data show a linear increase in group size, social scientists should certainly be interested in investigating the cause.

FINDINGS ON COALITIONS

Several important findings about the impact of the presence of a terrorist coalition on the transnational terrorist act have also been discussed. The most important of these findings are:

- Deaths are more likely to result from negotiated terrorist acts when a coalition is present.
- Injuries are more likely to result from negotiated terrorist acts when a coalition is present.
- The average numbers of deaths and injuries are greater when a coalition is present.

- Coalitional activity varies from year to year as a result of specific joint campaigns carried out from time to time.
- Coalitional activity was highest during the period from 1972 through 1975.
- Coalitions are more likely than single groups to commit difficult or moderately difficult acts as opposed to simple hit-and-run acts. This finding gives credence to the argument that most coalitions involve one group helping another in the commission of a terrorist act which the latter would be unable to commit individually.
- Eastern Europe, Africa, and Asia are relatively immune to coalitional activity.
- North America, Latin America, Western Europe, and the Middle East all have significant levels of coalitional activity.
- Coalitional activity overall is comparatively rare, accounting for only 5.6 percent of all transnational terrorist acts.
- Coalitions generally have a short life span. During the period covered by the data, 73.5 percent of all coalitions lasted for only one act of terrorism, and only 10.3 percent survived for four or more acts.
- Seven coalitions became working partnerships by committing four or more acts together.
- Some groups were more prone to engage in coalitional activity than were others. Overall, 11 groups were each involved in five or more coalitional acts.

These findings raise several issues for the understanding of terrorist coalitions. For example, they offer some indication of the internal behavior of coalitions. Specifically, when a coalition commits a negotiated act of transnational terrorism, there is a greater likelihood that the outcome of the event will be violent than if a single group acts alone. This can be accounted for by the internal processes of bargaining in the terrorist group. When a coalition commits an act of terrorism and negotiates its demands, negotiation must take place between the terrorists and the authorities and between the groups involved as well. Since it is unlikely that two terrorist groups will have complete coincidence of interests, the chances of obtaining internal agreement for a coalition are much less than for a single group.

A second contributing factor may include the risk premium which the authorities must pay in order to secure a peaceful outcome for the event. The risk premium must be high enough to satisfy the minimum utility function of at least two groups. An example may help to clarify this explanation.

Assume that two groups have formed a coalition and have occupied an office building, taking several office workers as hostages. They threaten to kill all of the hostages and then blow up the building if their demands are not met. Group one demands that some payment be made, which we will call x_1. Group two demands a payment as well, x_2. If group one acted alone, the demand would be x_1. If group two acted alone, x_2 would be the demand. Together, however, the demand equals $x_1 + x_2$, or the greater of x_1 or x_2, depending on circumstances. Furthermore, assume that group one is willing to settle for some lesser amount, the risk premium, equal to $x_1 - y_1$. Similarly, group two will settle for $x_2 - y_2$. Thus, if group one acted alone the risk premium would be $x_1 - y_1$, and if group two were the only group involved it would be $x_2 - y_2$. However, since they are acting together, the premium is $P = (x_1 - y_1) + (x_2 - y_2)$. And P is usually greater than $x_1 - y_1$ or $x_2 - y_2$.

Bargaining with a coalition is thus more costly and more likely to end in a violent outcome. It is harder for the coalition to reach internal agreement and more difficult for the authorities to pay the necessary risk premium.

It is interesting to note that the internal bargaining process did not prevent coalitions from being able to complete an act of terrorism after it had been started. There were no differences between coalitions and single groups in terms of being able to carry the act to logistical completion. In all likelihood, internal disagreements and a lack of sufficient common interests would prevent two groups from even beginning an act. That is, incompatibility would make it impossible for them to even agree to the conditions for the commission of the act.

Previous studies have made the suggestion that coalitions generally are made up of two or more groups involved in the commission of an act which one or more of the groups lacks the resources to commit on its own. This does appear to be the case. Coalitions are not necessarily equal partnerships. They may be a form of aid by one group to another. This finding does not change the fact that most terrorist acts, whether a coalition is present or not, are simple, hit-and-run acts. Nonetheless, coalitions are more likely than single groups to commit moderately difficult or difficult acts of terrorism. The association between the presence of coalitions and the difficulty of the act, however, is modest.

An important finding of this study is that coalitions generally are regional occurrences. Some regions have significant coalitional activity and others have negligible coalitional activity. The reasons for this are not known. In all likelihood it depends on the number and kinds of terrorist groups operating within a region, as well as the specific issues and goals around which coalitions could be formed. If there are many groups with similar ideological orientations, then the potential for coalitional activity exists. If few groups exist, or there are no groups with similar goals, then the potential for coalition formation is much less. If there is no similarity of interest between the groups in a coalition, there must be some other motive which brings them together. However, it is doubtful that a coalition could carry out an act and coordinate its demands if there were not some common interest among them.

Coalitional activity, although it does vary somewhat, is still rare. Coalitions account for less than 6 percent of all transnational terrorist events, and in no region do they account for more than 6.8 percent of all terrorist acts.

This study has also shown that coalitional activity varies from year to year. It did not, however, increase in a linear fashion during the period under consideration. In most years very few coalitional acts occurred. However, during 1972, 1973, 1974, and 1975, elevated levels of coalitional activity appeared. This rise seems to be the result of a small number of very active coalitions that carried out joint campaigns during those years and then disbanded. In 1976 the level of coalitional activity returned to its pre-1972 level. The level of coalitional activity for a given period of time is thus dependent on whether or not significant joint campaigns occur during the period. There is no regular or linear pattern to the frequency of coalitional activity.

Most coalitions were also found to be of short duration. As "offensive alliances," they were formed, carried out their mission (usually a single act of terrorism), and were terminated. Most coalitions apparently did not have interests which were sufficiently alike to warrant the formation of long-term partnerships. In some instances, however, working partnerships were formed. None of these partnerships, as far as can be determined, lasted for more than seven acts, however.

An examination of coalitional activity year by year seems to indicate that even working partnerships were of short duration. Most committed all of their coalitional terrorist acts in a short span of time and then committed no further acts together. Thus, there do not appear to be long-term partnerships among terrorist organizations. This would tend to indicate, in contrast to what some authors would like to believe, that terrorist organizations do not cooperate as often or as closely as is often supposed. Cooperation in the terrorist act is an ad hoc occurrence. No "terrorist international" exists.

Those who postulate the existence of an "international terrorist conspiracy" masterminded by a single group or nation are seeking single-cause explanations for a complex phenomenon. Many coalitions have formed. Most have lasted only a short time, and there is no evidence that one group or one nation is behind the phenomenon of transnational terrorism. Indeed, there does not appear to be a commonality of interests among terrorist groups sufficient for them to form a single alliance. Even if one were to assume that the Eastern Bloc controls significant numbers of terrorist groups, one would have to explain those acts of terrorism that are aimed at Eastern Bloc nations and their clients. One must suppose that there are enough political causes, economic desires, and violent personalities to support terrorist groups of many ideological orientations.

SOCIAL SCIENCE THEORY AND
TRANSNATIONAL TERRORISM

Transnational Terrorism and the
International System

In Chapter 2 the effects of transnational terrorism on the international system and on the individual states within the system were discussed. Some of the more important effects are listed below.

- Terrorists do not respect national boundaries (Chalfont, 1982: 313).
- Transnational terrorists have significant relations with other terrorist organizations (Chalfont, 1982: 313).
- Transnational terrorism may be supported by a state (Chalfont, 1982: 313).
- Modern communications systems give transnational terrorism added importance because their demands and actions are seen and heard around the world, i.e., they may affect distant actors (Redlick, 1979: 85).
- Terrorism poses a crisis for democratic governments because their ability to respond is limited (Dror, 1983: 90).
- Terrorism is an issue for which no international response has been formulated (Kupperman and Trent, 1979: 141).
- The mass media give added significance to terrorism by providing an audience, which is necessary to the terrorist's plans (Wardlaw, 1982: 25; Milbank, 1978: 60).
- Transnational terrorism demonstrates that state boundaries can be penetrated easily by hostile forces without the consent of the state (Hutchison, 1975: 114-116).
- Transnational terrorism demonstrates the ability of small groups to harm the interests of a state (Hutchison, 1975: 114-116).
- Terrorism is disruptive to the international system (Hutchison, 1975: 114-116).
- Terrorism has gained international recognition and attention (Hutchison, 1975: 114-116).
- Terrorism demonstrates the ineffectiveness of strategic power (Hutchison, 1975: 114-116).

- Terrorism demonstrates the interdependence of the international system (Hutchison, 1975: 114–116).
- Terrorism undermines the authority of the state (Hutchison, 1975: 114-116).
- Terrorism often affects foreign entities in a particular area, e.g., corporations (Hutchison, 1975: 114-116).
- Transnational terrorism demonstrates the vulnerability of a technologically dependent world (Hutchison, 1975: 114-116).

These effects on other actors in the international system demonstrate that transnational terrorists do constitute a significant group of actors in the international system. However, they are not nation-states and therefore a state-centric view of the world system ignores their impact. The study of military conflict and ordinary diplomacy between states yields no information about this significant group of nonstate actors. A view which accepts many types of actors as playing a role is clearly necessary to understand the international system.

In this work an argument has been made that transnational terrorist groups constitute a class of significant actors in the international system. Moreover, their behavior has been studied from the perspective of exchange-based theories of political interest groups. This is done in order to relate transnational terrorist groups to the existing body of political science theory. The success of this theory as an explanation is discussed later in this chapter.

This study has also pointed out some of the policy implications of group size and terrorist coalitions. These findings are significant insofar as they present new information relevant to decision makers who are charged with the control of terrorism.

A great deal of attention has been given in this study to transnational terrorist coalitions. Specifically, their behavior has been studied through available data. This is significant in that it presents solid evidence about the behavior of a particular type of subnational coalition in the international system. Subnational coalitions are likely to become more and more important given the increasing number of issues which cut across national boundaries and the growth of nongovernmental actors in the international system. The behavior of alliances between nations remains an important aspect of international relations; however, attention must also be given to empirical studies of coalitions whose membership includes organizations that are not states. This study has made a step in that direction with the study of transnational terrorist coalitions.

Much more work is needed before the findings presented here about transnational terrorist coalitions can be generalized to all subnational coalitions, if they can be at all. However, this study does suggest several questions which should be addressed by future studies of subnational coalitions:

- What type of agreements are necessary for coalitions to operate?
- Are most coalitions of short duration?
- Is similarity of interests the only factor affecting coalition formation, or do other factors, such as selective incentives, have an effect?
- Are there some entities (organizations, persons, ideological orientations) who are significantly more likely to join coalitions than others? That is, do some organizations act strictly as loners while others cooperate and make trade-offs?
- What factors, including size, ideological diversity, etc., have an effect on coalition performance?
- What factors affect the duration of coalitions?
- How are coalitions governed?

This study has focused on only one type of subnational coalition. Transnational terrorists, however, are significant actors in the international system. Transnational terrorist coalitions are an important type of subnational coalition. Whether the behavior of terrrorist coalitions is like that of other subnational coalitions remains to be seen.

In the present work, an empirical study has been carried out in order to understand the role of two key variables in the transnational terrorist act. The findings of this study provide information on the behavior of a significant category of nonstate actors in the international system. Some of the effects of the size of the acting group of transnational terrorists and the presence of terrorist coalitions on the act of terrorism have been illuminated. Some of the findings were predicted during the generation of the hypotheses. Others were contrary to expectations. Thus, like many social science research efforts, this one demonstrated that the original theory did not predict correctly in all cases. Variables which the theory did not account for undoubtedly exist and affect the behavior of terrorists.

Nonetheless, the findings of this work constitute new information about the behavior of important actors in the international system. The question which must be addressed next is: Do rational choice and interest group theories constitute a theoretical orientation sufficient for the understanding of transnational terrorism?

RATIONAL CHOICE THEORY AND
TRANSNATIONAL TERRORISM

Rational choice theory and exchange theories of interest groups are predicated on the assumption that the actors under consideration are rational. Here, economic rationality is the issue. Briefly, to refresh our understanding, economic rationality assumes that an actor, faced with a choice of possible outcomes, will have a set of transitive preferences. That is, he will always choose the outcome which he prefers, i.e., the one which maximizes his positive utility or minimizes his negative utility. The actor will then act in such a manner as he believes is consistent with the attainment of the desired outcome.[3]

Whether terrorists are rational or not depends in part on the motives and goals which they have. It must be remembered that rationality, as the term is used in this study, exists only at the individual level. There can be no group goals and no group rationality except those of its members. Let us assume that the goal of a terrorist group is strictly financial. Its members simply desire to make money. In this case they would be rational actors if they committed acts of extortionate terrorism, e.g., bank robberies, diplomatic kidnappings, etc.

If the goals of the terrorists were strictly political, then they would be rational if they committed acts of terrorism which allow political bargaining and which draw media attention to their demands. It is quite likely that an act, or even several acts, of terrorism will not achieve the goals of the transnational terrorist group. The success of their efforts, however, is not really an issue. The question is, did they act in such a manner as they believed to be consistent with the attainment of their preferred outcome? In most cases, it can be argued, transnational terrorists do act rationally.

Two other aspects of utility maximization enter the picture at this point: risk and cost. One must consider what risks a terrorist group faces. For example, what are the chances of the group or some of its members being killed, captured, or wounded? If the chances are very high, then the risk may be so great as to make the act nonrational. Whether the risk renders the act nonrational depends upon the costs associated with the risk. These elements can be placed into a cost-benefit calculation by the terrorists to determine if the act is worthwhile. For example, if the terrorists calculate that the act has a .5 probability of being successful, that success (in terms of achieved goals) is worth 100 utility points, that there is a .5 probability that the act will fail and they will be captured, and that failure represents a loss of 150 utility points, then the act has a negative expected value. That is, the expected value of the act is $.5(100) - .5(150) = -.25$. It would not be rational for the group to commit this act because the cost-benefit calculation reveals that it is inconsistent with their preferred outcome.

Most terrorists are neither economists nor political scientists. It is therefore unlikely that they would carry out a formal cost-benefit analysis of every act they consider committing. Nonetheless, if they are like most actors, they will informally calculate their expected rewards, risks, and costs, and act accordingly. As pointed out earlier, such an analysis does not preclude the possibility that a given terrorist or group may have a preference for being killed and act in a manner that is likely to end in their death. At this point, it appears that transnational terrorists are basically rational actors.

In deference to those who prefer to view terrorists as "crazies," it can be pointed out that rationality has nothing to do with sanity. The former is strictly an analytical construction of economic understanding, the latter is a judgment of the actor's mental state. The two are not necessarily related. However, it seems that rationality theory is more likely to lead to an understanding of terrorist behavior than is the subjective assessment of their sanity.

Yet another aspect of rationality is the possibility of actions other than terrorism in pursuit of the goals of a group. To determine whether terrorism is the course most likely to maximize the utility of a group, one must consider the possibility of other activities. Are there legal means of action which may be successful? Does the group have the talent and resources to participate in other activities? Whether other activities exist depends on a variety of factors. In some regimes, for example, one can attempt to influence policy through the use of lobbying activities. In other regimes, such activities are illegal and there may be no peaceful forms of participation. It may also be the case that a certain group lacks the skills and financial resources needed to be influential in a legal manner. Knowing little about how terrorist decision making is carried out, we do not know which groups consider what alternative activities. However, the possibility of other activities must be taken into account.

Another question must be considered: is it rational for an individual to participate in transnational terrorism? Presumably, if enough individuals have combined to form a group and commit an act of terrorism, those individuals must believe that they are deriving some utility from the act. Before the rationality of participating in terrorism can be determined, an individual must consider several factors. First, the actor must consider whether or not he will be better off if the goals of the group are attained. If the individual's position will not change substantially either way, then there is no reason to participate unless some other inducement is offered. The other inducement is usually referred to as selective incentives. An actor may join a group whose goals are a matter of indifference to him at best if he can receive personally some benefit which he could not obtain outside the group. An individual could join a terrorist group in the hope of obtaining a high government position if the group succeeded in overthrowing the current regime. A terrorist may also derive satisfaction from the adventure of terrorism. Moreover, a terrorist may get significant utility from the financial gains of the group. That is, he may be in it for the money.

A second consideration enters the individual's calculus. The risks and costs to the individual, e.g., death or jail, must be weighed against the benefits of the collective goods the group seeks and whatever selective incentives the individual obtains.

Third, the individual must consider, if the collective goals of the group are his driving force, the probability that his activity will make a difference in the outcome. If it will not, the actor may be taking significant risks without any payoff.

If most terrorist groups are successful in obtaining their goals and those goals take the form of collective public goods, it would not be rational for an individual to participate in terrorism, as Tullock (1971) and Salert (1976) point out. The individual will share in the benefit whether he participates in its supply or not. Therefore, selective incentives may play a larger role in the formation and maintenance of terrorist groups than is often supposed. Many previous scholars have treated terrorists as simply ideologues or insane individuals bent on destruction. While it is true that most terrorists are probably committed to their cause, there are others similarly committed to an ideology who would never join a terrorist group. The role of selective incentives in attracting terrorists to the group requires further investigation.

Intuitively, it seems that a terrorist may be attracted by a combination of benefits. Moe (1980), in discussing ordinary interest groups, argues that a potential member will join if the sum of the utility the actor derives from the collective goals of the group, selective economic incentives, and solidary benefits is greater than the costs of participation. Potential terrorist group members probably perform the same type of calculation. Thus, terrorist activity may result from a combination of factors having nothing to do with the sanity of the participants, and some of which have nothing to do with the political goals of the group.

The role of selective incentives has been largely ignored in the previous literature on terrorism.[4] The reason for this is, partly, that scholars of terrorism are often convinced that terrorism is something vastly different from other political processes and that terrorist organizations are not political organizations in the ordinary sense. Others view terrorists as simply criminals or lunatics. However, selective incentives may play a significant role and should be considered. Terrorists can be studied as rational individuals.

The study of terrorists as rational individuals does not presume that they have perfect information and will, in all cases, succeed in maximizing their personal utility. The approach assumes that they will do their best to maximize their utility under the given circumstances. In short, terrorists are viewed as calculating actors who take into account the costs and benefits of their activities before acting. Thus, they may commit acts of terrorism when they believe it is to their benefit and act in other ways when terrorism is too costly or not beneficial enough. Of course, ideological orientations play a significant role in the individual's decision to join a terrorist organization. However, ideology is only one of several factors. The rational approach assumes that personal cost-benefit calculations will be largely responsible for separating those people with the same ideology into terrorists and nonterrorists.

In this study an attempt has been made to treat terrorist organizations as political interest groups. This attempt is predicated on the belief that it is possible to advance our understanding of terrorism by extending an existing theory. Our knowledge is not sufficient to allow us to be sure what approach offers the best explanation. However, existing theories should be tested before social scientists assume that the phenomenon of transnational terrorism requires a new theory of its own. Indeed, when terrorists are referred to as "crazies" the author is really substituting his own ideology for solid theory. Such attempts to define a phenomenon solely on the basis of ideology should not be allowed to influence objective scholarship.

Are terrorist organizations political interest groups? In this study an assumption has been made that they can be studied as interest groups because their political goals often take the form of public goods. Following Olson's (1971: 5-6) argument, this study assumed that terrorist groups exist to further the common interests of their members. They seek public goods and, therefore, they are political interest groups.

The question now is: does the rational choice (exchange) theory of interest groups offer a sufficient basis for the study of transnational terrorism? The answer depends on two factors: whether the exchange theory is sufficient for understanding interest groups at all and whether or not transnational terrorist groups are sufficiently like other interest groups to be explained by the same theory. In this work several hypotheses were presented based on rational choice theories of interest groups. Some of these hypotheses turned out to be consistent with the data and others did not. Thus, the conclusion of this study is that it is not clear whether this theory will turn out to be an adequate theory for understanding transnational terrorism. A good deal of further work on other aspects of the theory needs to be done before its status can be determined.

Several possibilities exist in regard to the status of the theory. First, it may not be adequate to explain the behavior of any political interest group.[5] A second possibility is that the theory is adequate for most interest groups, but that terrorist groups are so different from other political organizations that the theory does not apply to them. A third possibility is that the theory is adequate and that further work will yield propositions based on the theory which will satisfactorily explain transnational terrorism. Whatever the outcome of future studies using rational choice understandings of interest groups, at least an effort must be made to find a theory which does explain transnational terrorism. At this point the status of the theory under consideration cannot be determined. This does not seem an unusual conclusion since this is the first effort to apply the theory to terrorism and to test it using data.

FUTURE STUDIES OF TRANSNATIONAL TERRORISM

At the present there are no widely accepted theories of transnational terrorism and, thus, there is a great deal of work remaining. It should be noted that the lack of a widely accepted theory is not an unusual problem in the social sciences.

Future research efforts must first be cognizant of the need for a clear, precise, and ideologically neutral operational definition of terrorism. Many studies have proceeded with no clear definition in mind. Others have allowed their ideological biases to influence their definition.[6] Yet another group of authors is unclear about what constitutes terrorism in terms of types of violence. The term may be used to refer to all violence, whatever the purpose, or it may be used indiscriminately to define all political violence aimed at current authorities. The latter may make no distinction between terrorism and insurgent attacks on military targets.

In future studies, analysts should at least be explicit as to what, for purposes of the study, constitutes terrorism. Although the definition can be changed from one study to another, it should at least be stated clearly. The study of terrorism cannot advance rapidly if one researcher does not know whether or not another is even discussing the same subject. Moreover, operational definitions must be formulated without regard to ideology or the personal preferences of the researcher. Operational definitions should delimit the field of study, not support a particular point of view.

Future studies of terrorism in general and transnational terrorism in particular must begin from an informed theoretical point of view. They may attempt to fit terrorism to a previously existing theory, as this study has done, or they can begin with a new theory. The advancement of our understanding, however, requires that a study should begin with some theoretical orientation. Many studies have begun without any theory whatsoever. This is especially true of studies of trends, frequencies, and chronologies of terrorism. Such studies have value in terms of pointing out the activities of terrorists which may lead to theorizing. Moreover, they are crucial to studies of risk analysis in terrorism. However, they do little to advance our understanding of the phenomenon.

It should be noted that the data used in this study is itself essentially chronological data. This is the case with most events data collection efforts. However, the fact that data collection is conducted on the basis of sequential events does not preclude the use of the data for other purposes. Even though the data may be collected without reference to a specific theory, if the data are sufficient they can be used for theoretically based studies. The problems are not much different from those faced by any researcher who conducts secondary analysis using data collected with the aid of a theory other than his own.

A theoretical orientation can provide the questions which guide the study of transnational terrorism. Several questions that may result from a solid theoretical orientation are listed below.

- What is transnational terrorism? How are we to define it?
- What type of actors are transnational terrorists? Nonstate actors, quasi-states, interest groups, etc.?
- What behaviors does the theory predict for terrorists?
- Are terrorists a normal type of political actor, or are they a completely new class of their own?

A theory should inform the entire study of transnational terrorism. It shapes the questions to be investigated and allows the development of testable hypotheses. True, hypotheses can be generated and tested without reference to a theory; however, when this is done the meaning of the results of the hypothesis testing is unknown. Explanation and understanding require that statistically significant findings be theoretically significant as well. Whether the tests reveal that the data is consistent or inconsistent with the theory, knowledge will be advanced. If the data is consistently at variance with the hypotheses generated by the theory, at least the number of possible theories for explaining transnational terrorism will be reduced. Given the number of theories in the social sciences which could be applied to terrorism, this would be an important achievement.

Future studies of transnational terrorism should also seek, whenever possible, to test the propositions developed in other studies. Many studies make statements about transnational terrorism which are not supported by any solid evidence. Researchers should seek to test the statements of other scholars rather than repeat them indiscriminately.

Jenkins (1979) is right in pointing out another area for further research on transnational terrorism, i.e., how terrorists make decisions. Virtually no information is currently available which is supported by empirical evidence on how terrorist groups are organized and how they make decisions. For example, we know little about how terrorist organization leaders achieve their positions. We do not know if all acting groups have a leader or if some may have no authority structure. Such a distinction can be very important at the operational level in that it can affect who the authorities must negotiate with, e.g., a single leader or an entire group.

Social scientists also know very little about how terrorist leaders maintain their positions of authority. In short, terrorist leaders present an interesting and completely uncharted subject group for the study of political leadership and political recruitment. It may be possible to gather some of the information necessary for studies in this field from interviews with captured terrorists.

Theoretical work on transnational terrorism, regardless of which aspect is studied, may be undertaken in several ways. Two of the most important techniques are deductive work and empirical observation.

Most rational choice studies of terrorism, like many rational choice studies in general, are deductive works. The researcher sets forth an axiom or set of axioms.[7] From the axioms, certain suppositions about behavior are derived. The scholar then sets out to demonstrate the veracity of his expectations in a logical or mathematical manner. Such study is basically an intuitive and deductive exercise, which demonstrates that if one accepts the axiom and the given set of conditions and constraints, then certain propositions will be verified. It is generally true that if one accepts the conditions, the outcome follows.

These studies are important in that they provide a logical understanding of a phenomenon. They may also predict behavior under certain conditions. Theoretically, they are important because they force the scholar to rigorously define his subject and set forth the initial conditions. They require the scholar to theorize. In this way they may generate solid theories for the understanding of transnational terrorism. They may also generate testable propositions about the subject. However, such studies do not test their propositions empirically.

Empirical studies are therefore needed. An empirical study could even start with deductive work. One could test the propositions under the given conditions, and even test the axiom itself if suitable data can be found. Thus, deductive and empirical studies can be complementary.

Empirical work, however, is required for another reason. It allows an examination of the evidence and leads to a greater understanding of transnational terrorism whether the hypotheses are supported or not. Moreover, empirical studies allow for the testing of propositions and statements about terrorism made by other scholars. Simply stating that something is the case does not make it so. The evidence must be examined before such statements become part of the accepted "knowledge"of a discipline. Empirical work, particularly data-based studies, is needed to advance our understanding. The hypotheses generated by a theory must be subject to testing. Such testing allows us to refine the theory and generate further hypotheses. A theory is necessary, but so is evidence. The theorist and the empiricist, although they may be the same person, must work together to further our understanding.

Future studies of terrorism are going to require enhanced data-gathering efforts. The usable data on transnational terrorism is limited to a very few data sets. The ITERATE data set, the most comprehensive data set available, focuses on the transnational terrorist act. Its observations consist of event characteristics. Little data is presented on the groups or individual terrorists. It is suitable for some types of studies, but not for others.

Data-gathering efforts in the future can take several directions. First, it is important that the data on transnational terrorist events be extended to cover later years. Second, data should be gathered systematically on transnational terrorist organizations. The whole organization should be the focus: what type of events does it initiate? How often? How many members? What is the age distribution? The educational distribution? What type of leadership and decision-making structures exist? What is the group's ideological orientation?

Such questions as those presented above would allow us to study how the overall organizational characteristics of the group affect its activities. Currently, such data is available for very few groups, and it is rarely more than a rough estimation. Of course, an effort to gather organizational data will be difficult. Authoritative membership figures are probably not available. However, interviews have been conducted with captured terrorists. Such interviews usually focus on the terrorists themselves. They could be used to derive whatever information is known to terrorists about the group itself. If nothing else, scholars could undertake case studies of several groups in depth and compare them even if quantitative data is not available.

More data is also needed on individual terrorists. However, so far the interviews have been concerned mainly with demographic variables. Ideology and personality should be probed more deeply, if possible. It is important that social scientists understand what type of individual becomes a terrorist and what attracts him. Is the attraction political? Selective incentives? Adventure? Violent personality? These questions are crucial to our understanding of terrorism as a political phenomenon.

In short, broad-based, stepped-up data-gathering efforts are needed to advance our understanding of transnational terrorism. While such undertakings pose several problems, it is important that we attempt to overcome them.

In this study an attempt has been made to understand transnational terrorist organizations as nonstate actors in the international system and as political interest groups. A rational choice approach to interest groups has been used as the basis for developing propositions about two key variables (group size and the presence of coalitions) and their operational consequences at the level of the transnational terrorist act. Some of these propositions have been supported by the evidence, others have not. This study must conclude that, at this point, it cannot be determined whether or not rational choice theory generally, or interest group theory in particular, will prove to be a suitable approach to transnational terrorism. A great deal of further work must be done before that determination can be made.

Aside from the hypothesis testing, this study has accomplished several objectives. It has presented a way of fitting transnational terrorism into models of the international system, i.e., as nonstate actors and political interest groups. Previous quantitative studies of terrorism have been reviewed systematically. A discussion of previous writings on group size and coalitions has also been presented. This literature has not been previously collated as a body.

This work has also discussed several possible definitions and typologies of terrorism in general and transnational terrorism in particular. A study of possible definitions is necessary for any scholar to understand exactly what constitutes terrorism.

The work reported here has not demonstrated that rational choice is a sufficient basis for a general theory of transnational terrorism. Nonetheless, the data analysis, literature reviews, and theory construction together make a significant contribution to the advancement of our understanding of transnational terrorism.

NOTES

1. Much of the literature on personalities is discussed by Oots and Wiegele (1985).

2. The recent suicide bombings of peacekeeping forces in Lebanon may be an example of single actor, extreme violence explained by ideology. Certainly, an uncompromising devotion to a cause was required to justify, in the minds of the bombers, the killing of large numbers of soldiers, not to mention the loss of one's own life.

3. Rational choice theory does not attempt to assess rationality in terms of which outcomes are preferred. Rather, it concerns itself with whether or not the actors behave in a manner consistent with their preferences. For example, the recent "suicide bombers" in Lebanon apparently had a desire to be martyred for their cause and thereby go directly to heaven. According to rational choice theory, they were behaving in a rational manner because they were acting in a way which was consistent with their desire for martyrdom. It is apparent that in its simplest form, rational choice theory can be a tautological

theory. If an actor behaves in a certain manner one can simply state that he is being rational because he must have preferred the outcome he attempted to obtain or he would not have acted in that manner. Such an argument is tautological and trivial. The theory has meaning only as a prospective theory. That is, preferences must be established first, and then behavior observed to see if it follows from the initial assumptions.

4. Tullock (1971) and Salert (1976) are general exceptions to this. However, they were interested in the broader question of revolution rather than the narrower issue of terrorism specifically.

5. It should be noted that Olson (1971), Moe (1980), Salisbury (1969), Frohlich, Oppenheimer, and Young (1971), and others who have used this approach to interest groups have done so mainly from a deductive approach. Their conclusions are logical given their axioms. However, except for Moe (1980), no data is presented to test any of the propositions.

6. Plainly, those who believe that all terrorism is the product of the Soviet bloc have this problem as do those who assume the existence of a "terrorist international." Such studies presume that terrorism must begin from a left-wing ideology, which is contrary to the evidence. Dobson and Payne (1982: 183), for example, note that in West Germany there are approximately 20,000 members and about 1,800 activists in extreme right-wing and neo-Nazi groups. Notably, the Wehrsportgruppe Hoffman is an active neo-Nazi terrorist group which perpetrates acts of political violence on Germany's Jewish population. Hoffman (1982) should be consulted for a good, general treatment of right-wing terrorism.

Terrorist groups may thus be right or left politically. They can also be organized around a number of other attributes including religion. There are terrorist groups whose members are Jewish (e.g., the Jewish Defense League), Roman Catholic (e.g., IRA), and Protestant (e.g., Ulster Defense Association). There is no single attribute, issue, or ideology around which terrorist groups form. The issues and attributes which form the basis for terrorist action are as diverse as those motivating other forms of political participation.

7. Riker (1962: 7) states that an axiom is a statement about what reality is like from which nonobvious propositions can be derived and tested. The axiom itself, however, receives its justification on intuitive grounds.

BIBLIOGRAPHY

Adeniran, Tunde, and Yonah Alexander, eds. 1983. *International Violence*. New York: Praeger.

Alexander, Yonah, ed. 1976. *International Terrorism: National, Regional, and Global Perspectives*. New York: Praeger.

Alexander, Yonah, David Carlton, and Paul Wilkinson, eds. 1979. *Terrorism: Theory and Practice*. Boulder, Colorado: Westview Press.

Alexander, Yonah, and Seymour Maxwell Finger, eds. 1977. *Terrorism: Interdisciplinary Perspectives*. New York: The John Jay Press.

Alexander, Yonah, and John M. Gleason, eds. 1981. *Behavioral and Quantitative Perspectives on Terrorism*. New York: Pergamon Press.

Alexander, Yonah, and Robert A. Kilmarx. 1979a. "International Network of Terrorist Movements." In *Political Terrorism and Business: The Threat and Response*, edited by Yonah Alexander and Robert A. Kilmarx, 34-55. New York: Praeger.

Alexander, Yonah, and Robert A. Kilmarx, eds. 1979b. *Political Terrorism and Business: The Threat and Response*. New York: Praeger.

Amos, John W., II, and Russell H. S. Stolfi. 1982. "Controlling International Terrorism: Alternatives Palatable and Unpalatable." *Annals of the American Academy of Political and Social Science* 463 (September): 69-83 (Marvin E. Wolfgang, issue editor).

Anable, David. 1978. "Terrorism." In *Contemporary Terrorism: Selected Readings*, edited by John D. Elliot and Leslie K. Gibson, 247-259. Gaithersburg, Maryland: International Association of Chiefs of Police.

Avery, William P. 1981. "Terrorism, Violence, and the International Transfer of Conventional Armaments." In *Behavioral and Quantitative Perspectives on Terrorism*, edited by Yonah Alexander and John M. Gleason, 329-342. New York: Pergamon Press.

Bass, Gail, and Brian Michael Jenkins. 1983. *A Review of Recent Trends in International Terrorism and Nuclear Incidents Abroad*. Santa Monica, California: Rand Corporation. Research Note, N1979-SL.

Beer, Francis A. 1981. *Peace against War: The Ecology of International Violence*. San Francisco: W. H. Freeman and Company.

Bell, J. Bowyer. 1971. "Contemporary Revolutionary Organizations." *International Organization* 25, no. 3 (Summer): 503-518 (Joseph S. Nye and Robert O. Keohane, guest editors).

Bell, J. Bowyer. 1975. *Transnational Terror*. Washington and Stanford: AEI-Hoover.

Bell, J. Bowyer. 1978a. "Terror: An Overview." In *International Terrorism in the Contemporary World*, edited by Marius H. Livingston, with Lee Bruce Kress and Marie G. Wanek, 36-43. Westport, Connecticut: Greenwood Press.

Bell, J. Bowyer. 1978b. *A Time of Terror. How Democratic Societies Respond to Revolutionary Violence*. New York: Basic Books.

Bertelsen, Judy S. 1977a. "An Introduction to the Study of Nonstate Nations in International Politics." In *Nonstate Nations in International Politics: Comparative System Analysis*, edited by Judy S. Bertelsen, 1-5. New York: Praeger.

Bertelsen, Judy S. 1977b. "The Nonstate Nation in International Politics: Some Observations." In *Nonstate Nations in International Politics: Comparative System Analysis*, edited by Judy S. Bertelsen, 245-257. New York: Praeger.

Bertelsen, Judy S., ed. 1977c. *Nonstate Nations in International Politics: Comparative System Analysis*. New York: Praeger.

Blalock, Hubert M. 1979. *Social Statistics*. 2d ed. New York: McGraw-Hill.

Bonanate, Luigi. 1979. "Terrorism and International Political Analysis." *Terrorism: An International Journal* 3, nos. 1/2: 47-67.

Buchanan, James M. 1968. *The Demand and Supply of Public Goods*. Chicago: Rand McNally.

Buchanan, James M., and Gordon Tullock. 1965. *The Calculus of*

Consent: Logical Foundations of Constitutional Democracy. Ann
Arbor: University of Michigan Press.

Carlton, David. 1979. "The Future of Political Substate Violence." In
Terrorism: Theory and Practice, edited by Yonah Alexander,
David Carlton, and Paul Wilkinson, 201-230. Boulder, Colo-
rado: Westview Press.

Central Intelligence Agency. 1978. *International Terrorism in 1977.*
Washington, D.C.: Central Intelligence Agency.

Chalfont, The Right Honorable Lord. 1982. "Terrorism and International Security." *Terrorism: An International Journal* 5, no. 4:
309-323.

Chamberlin, John. 1974. "The Provision of Collective Goods as a
Function of Group Size." *American Political Science Review* 68:
707-716.

Clutterbuck, Richard. 1975. *Living with Terrorism.* London: Faber and
Faber.

Cooper, H. H. A. 1978a. "Terrorism and the Intelligence Function."
In *International Terrorism in the Contemporary World*, edited
by Marius H. Livingston, with Lee Bruce Kress, and Marie G.
Wanek, 287-296. Westport, Connecticut: Greenwood Press.

Cooper, H. H. A. 1978b. "Whither Now? Terrorism on the Brink." In
Contemporary Terrorism: Selected Readings, edited by John D.
Elliot and Leslie K. Gibson, 269-284. Gaithersburg, Maryland:
International Association of Chiefs of Police.

Cordes, Bonnie, Bruce Hoffman, Brian M. Jenkins, Konrad Kellen,
Sue Moran, and William Sater. 1984. *Trends in International
Terrorism, 1982 and 1983.* Santa Monica, California: Rand
Corporation. Report R-3183-SL.

Corsino, MacArthur Flores. 1977. "A Conceptual Framework for
Studying the International Relations of a Communist Revolu-
tionary Movement: The Partai Komunis Indonesia." Ph.D. diss.,
Northern Illinois University.

Crenshaw, Martha. 1981. "The Causes of Terrorism." *Comparative
Politics* 13, no. 4 (July): 379-399.

Crenshaw, Martha. 1983a. "Conclusions." In *Terrorism, Legitimacy
and Power: The Consequences of Political Violence*, edited by
Martha Crenshaw, 143-149. Middletown, Connecticut: Wesleyan University Press.

Crenshaw, Martha. 1983b. "The International Consequences of Terrorism." Paper presented to the American Political Science Association Annual Meeting, September 1-4, Chicago.

Crenshaw, Martha. 1983c. "Introduction: Reflections of the Effects of
Terrorism." In *Terrorism, Legitimacy and Power: The Conse-*

quences of Political Violence, edited by Martha Crenshaw, 1-37. Middletown, Connecticut: Wesleyan University Press.

Crenshaw, Martha, ed. 1983d. Terrorism, Legitimacy and Power: The Consequences of Political Violence. Middletown, Connecticut: Wesleyan University Press.

Demaris, Ovid. 1977. Brothers in Blood: The International Terrorist Network. New York: Charles Scribner's Sons.

Deutsch, Antal. 1982. "On the Economics of Terrorism." Terrorism: An International Journal 5, no. 4: 363-366.

Devine, Philip A., and Robert J. Rafalko. 1982. "On Terror." Annals of the American Academy of Political and Social Science 463 (September) (Marvin E. Wolfgang, issue editor): 39-53.

Dobson, Christopher, and Ronald Payne. 1982. The Terrorists: Their Weapons, Leaders and Tactics. rev. ed. New York: Facts on File, Inc.

Dobson, Douglas, James L. Franke, and Lloyd P. Jones. 1981. "The Problem of Representation in Interest Groups." Unpublished Manuscript, Northern Illinois University, DeKalb.

Downs, Anthony. 1957. An Economic Theory of Democracy. New York: Harper and Row.

Dror, Yehezkel. 1983. "Terrorism as a Challenge to the Democratic Capacity to Govern." In Terrorism, Legitimacy and Power: The Consequences of Political Violence, edited by Martha Crenshaw, 65-90. Middletown, Connecticut: Wesleyan University Press.

Duggard, John A. 1974. "International Terrorism: Problems of a Definition." International Affairs 50, no. 1 (January): 67-81.

Elliot, John D., and Leslie K. Gibson, eds. 1978. Contemporary Terrorism: Selected Readings. Gaithersburg, Maryland: International Association of Chiefs of Police.

Farrell, William Regis. 1982. The U.S. Government Response to Terrorism: In Search of an Effective Strategy. Boulder, Colorado: Westview Press.

Fearey, Robert A. 1978. "Introduction to Transnational Terrorism." In International Terrorism in the Contemporary World, edited by Marius H. Livingston, with Lee Bruce Kress, and Marie G. Wanek, 25-35. Westport, Connecticut: Greenwood Press.

Fenwick, Charles G. 1965. International Law. 4th ed. New York: Appleton-Century-Crofts.

Feierabend, Ivo K., Rosalind L. Feierabend, and Ted Robert Gurr, eds. 1972. Anger, Violence, and Politics: Theories and Research. Englewood Cliffs, New Jersey: Prentice-Hall, Inc.

Ferracuti, Franco. 1982. "A Sociopsychiatric Interpretation of Terrorism." *Annals of the American Academy of Political and Social Science* 463 (September) (Marvin E. Wolfgang, issue editor): 129–140.

Field, Werner. 1971. "Nongovernmental Entities in the International System." *Orbis* 15: 879-922.

Finger, Seymour Maxwell. 1976. "International Terrorism and the United Nations." In *International Terrorism: National, Regional, and Global Perspectives*, edited by Yonah Alexander, 323-348. New York: Praeger.

Finger, Seymour Maxwell. 1983. "Security of International Civil Aviation: The Role of the ICAO." *Terrorism: An International Journal* 6, no. 4 (Theme issue: United Nations Cooperation Against Terrorism; Amos Yoder, guest editor): 519-527.

Fitzgerald, Bruce D. 1978. "The Analytical Foundations of Extortionate Terrorism." *Terrorism: An International Journal* 1: 347-362.

Fox, William T. R., ed. 1959. *Theoretical Aspects of International Relations*. Notre Dame, Indiana: University of Notre Dame Press.

Fowler, William Warner. 1980. "An Agenda for Quantitative Research on Terrorism." Santa Monica, California: Rand Corporation. Paper, P-6591.

Friedlander, Robert A. 1977. "The Origins of International Terrorism." In *Terrorism: Interdisciplinary Perspectives*, edited by Yonah Alexander and Seymour Maxwell Finger, 30-45. New York: The John Jay Press.

Friedlander, Robert A. 1979. *Terrorism: Documents of International and Local Control*. 4 vols. Dobbs Ferry, New York: Oceana Publications, Inc.

Friedlander, Robert A. 1983. "The Psychology of Terrorism: Contemporary Views." In *Managing Terrorism: Strategies for the Corporate Executive*, edited by Patrick J. Montana and George S. Roukis, 41-54. Westport, Connecticut: Greenwood Press.

Frohlich, Norman, Richard Hunt, Joe A. Oppenheimer, and Richard E. Wagner. 1975. "Individual Contributions for Public Goods." *Journal of Conflict Resolution* 9: 310-329.

Frohlich, Norman, and Joe A. Oppenheimer. 1970. "I Get by with a Little Help from My Friends." *World Politics* 23: 104-120.

Frohlich, Norman, Joe A. Oppenheimer, and Oran R. Young. 1971. *Political Leadership and Collective Goods*. Princeton, New Jersey: Princeton University Press.

Fromkin, David. 1978. "The Strategy of Terrorism." In *Contemporary Terrorism: Selected Readings*, edited by John D. Elliot and Leslie K. Gibson, 11-24. Gaithersburg, Maryland: International Association of Chiefs of Police.

George, Alexander L. 1980. *Presidential Decisionmaking in Foreign Policy: The Effective Use of Information and Advice.* Boulder, Colorado: Westview Press.

Gleason, John M. 1980. "A Poisson Model of Incidents of International Terrorism in the United States." *Terrorism: An International Journal* 4, nos. 1/4: 259-265.

Gleason, John M. 1981. "Third World Terrorism: Perspectives for Quantitative Research." In *Behavioral and Quantitative Perspectives on Terrorism*, edited by Yonah Alexander and John M. Gleason, 242-255. New York: Pergamon Press.

Grabosky, P. N. 1979. "The Urban Context of Political Terrorism." In *The Politics of Terrorism*, edited by Michael Stohl, 51-76. New York: Marcel Dekker.

Gurr, Ted Robert. 1970. *Why Men Rebel.* Princeton, New Jersey: Princeton University Press.

Gurr, Ted Robert. 1972. "A Causal Model of Civil Strife: A Comparative Analysis Using New Indices." In *Anger, Violence, and Politics: Theories and Research*, edited by Ivo K. Feierabend, Rosalind L. Feierabend, and Ted Robert Gurr, 31-57. Englewood Cliffs, New Jersey: Prentice-Hall, Inc. Reprinted from the *American Political Science Review* 62, no. 4 (December 1968): 1104-1124.

Gurr, Ted Robert. 1979. "Some Characteristics of Political Terrorism in the 1960's." In *The Politics of Terrorism*, edited by Michael Stohl, 23-79. New York: Marcel Dekker.

Hacker, Frederick. 1976. *Crusaders, Criminals and Crazies: Terror and Terrorism in Our Time.* New York: W. W. Norton and Company.

Hamilton, Lawrence C. 1978a. "A Causal Theory of Terrorism." Paper presented to the Joint National Meeting of the Operations Research Society of America and the Institute of Management Sciences, May 1-3, New York.

Hamilton, Lawrence C. 1978b. "The Ecology of Terrorism: A Historical and Statistical Study." Ph.D. diss., University of Colorado.

Hamilton, Lawrence C. 1981. "Dynamics of Insurgent Violence: Preliminary Findings." In *Behavioral and Quantitative Perspectives on Terrorism*, edited by Yonah Alexander and John M. Gleason, 229-241. New York: Pergamon Press.

Hamilton, Lawrence C., and James D. Hamilton. 1983. "Dynamics of Terrorism." *International Studies Quarterly* 27, no. 1 (March): 39-54.

Heuer, Richards J., Jr., ed. 1978. *Quantitative Approaches to Politi-*

cal Intelligence: The CIA Experience. Boulder, Colorado: Westview Press.

Heyman, Edward S. 1980. "The Diffusion of Transnational Terrorism." In *Responding to the Terrorist Threat: Security and Crisis Management*, edited by Richard H. Shultz and Stephen Sloan, 190-244. New York: Pergamon Press.

Heyman, Edward, and Edward F. Mickolus. 1980. "Observations on Why Violence Spreads." *International Studies Quarterly* 24, no. 2 (June): 299-305.

Heyman, Edward, and Edward F. Mickolus. 1981. "Imitation by Terrorists: Quantitative Approaches to the Study of Diffusion Patterns in Transnational Terrorism." In *Behavioral and Quantitative Perspectives on Terrorism*, edited by Yonah Alexander and John M. Gleason, 175-228. New York: Pergamon Press.

Hilton, Gordon. n.d. "Risk Aversion and Terrorism." Unpublished Manuscript, Northern Illinois University, DeKalb.

Hoffman, Bruce. 1982. "Right-Wing Terrorism in Europe." Santa Monica, California: Rand Corporation. Note, N-1856-AF.

Holsti, Ole R., P. Terrance Hopmann, and John D. Sullivan. 1973. *Unity and Disintegration in International Alliances*. New York: John Wiley and Sons.

Holton, Gerald. 1978. "Reflections on Modern Terrorism." *Terrorism: An International Journal* 1, nos. 3/4: 265-276.

Hopple, Gerald W. 1982. "Transnational Terrorism: Prospectus for a Causal Modeling Approach." *Terrorism: An International Journal* 6, no. 1: 73-100.

Horowitz, Irving Louis. 1973. "Political Terrorism and State Power." *Journal of Political and Military Sociology* 1, no. 1 (Spring): 147-157.

Horowitz, Irving Louis. 1977. "Transnational Terrorism, Civil Liberties and Social Science." In *Terrorism: Interdisciplinary Perspectives*, edited by Yonah Alexander and Seymour Maxwell Finger, 283-297. New York: The John Jay Press.

Horowitz, Irving Louis. 1983. "The Routinization of Terrorism and Its Unanticipated Consequences." In *Terrorism, Legitimacy and Power: The Consequences of Political Violence*, edited by Martha Crenshaw, 38-51. Middletown, Connecticut: Wesleyan University Press.

Hubbard, David G. 1983. "The Psychodynamics of Terrorism." In *International Violence*, edited by Tunde Adeniran and Yonah Alexander, 43-53. New York: Praeger.

Huntington, Samuel P. 1973. "Transnational Organizations in World Politics." *World Politics* 25: 333-368.

Hutchison, Martha Crenshaw. 1975. "Transnational Terrorism and World Politics." *The Jerusalem Journal of International Relations* 1, no. 2 (Winter): 109-129.

Hyams, Edward. 1975. *Terrorists and Terrorism*. London: J. M. Dent and Sons, Ltd.

Jenkins, Brian Michael. 1976. "Hostage Survival: Some Preliminary Observations." Santa Monica, California: Rand Corporation. Paper, P-5627.

Jenkins, Brian Michael. 1978a. "International Terrorism: A Balance Sheet." In *Contemporary Terrorism: Selected Readings*, edited by John D. Elliot and Leslie K. Gibson, 235-245. Gaithersburg, Maryland: International Association of Chiefs of Police.

Jenkins, Brian Michael. 1978b. "International Terrorism: Trends and Potentialities." Santa Monica, California: Rand Corporation. Paper, P-6117.

Jenkins, Brian Michael. 1979. "The Terrorist Mindset and Terrorist Decision Making: Two Areas of Ignorance." Santa Monica, California: Rand Corporation. Paper, P-6340.

Jenkins, Brian Michael. 1980. "Terrorism in the 1980's." Santa Monica, California: Rand Corporation. Paper, P-6564.

Jenkins, Brian Michael. 1982a. "Diplomats on the Front Line." Santa Monica, California: Rand Corporation. Paper, P-6749.

Jenkins, Brian Michael. 1982b. "Statements about Terrorism." *Annals of the American Academy of Political and Social Science* 463 (September): 11-23 (Marvin E. Wolfgang, issue editor).

Jenkins, Brian Michael. 1982c. "Talking to Terrorists." Santa Monica, California: Rand Corporation. Paper, P-6750.

Jenkins, Brian Michael, and J. Johnson. 1975. *International Terrorism: A Chronology, 1968–1974*. Santa Monica, California: Rand Corporation. Report, R-1597.

Jenkins, Brian Michael, and J. Johnson. 1976. *International Terrorism: A Chronology*. 1974 supplement. Santa Monica, California: Rand Corporation. Report, R-1909-1.

Jenkins, Brian Michael, J. Johnson, and D. F. Ronfeldt. 1977. "Numbered Lives: Some Statistical Observations from 77 International Hostage Episodes." Santa Monica, California: Rand Corporation. Paper, P-5905.

Karber, Phillip A., and R. William Mengel. 1983. "Political and Economic Forces Affecting Terrorism." In *Managing Terrorism: Strategies for the Corporate Executive*, edited by Patrick J.

Montana and George S. Roukis, 23-40. Westport, Connecticut: Greenwood Press.

Keohane, Robert O., and Joseph S. Nye. 1974. "Transnational Relations and World Politics." *World Politics* 27: 39-62.

Kirk, Richard M. 1983. "Political Terrorism and the Size of Government: A Positive Institutional Analysis of Violent Political Strategy." *Public Choice* 40: 41-52.

Knauss, Peter R., and D. A. Strickland. 1979. "Political Disintegration and Latent Terror." In *The Politics of Terrorism*, edited by Michael Stohl, 77-117. New York: Marcel Dekker.

Knutson, Jeanne N. 1980. "The Terrorist's Dilemmas: Some Implicit Rules of the Game." *Terrorism: An International Journal* 4, nos. 1/4: 195-222.

Kupperman, Robert H. 1979. "The Threat: Some Technological Considerations." In *Political Terrorism and Business: The Threat and Response*, edited by Yonah Alexander and Robert A. Kilmarx, 3-11. New York: Praeger.

Kupperman, Robert H., and Darrell Trent, eds. 1979. *Terrorism: Threat, Reality, Response*. Stanford, California: Hoover Institution Press.

Kupperman, Robert H., with Debra Van Opstal, and David J. Williamson, Jr. 1982. "Terror, The Strategic Tool: Response and Control." *Annals of the American Academy of Political and Social Science* 463 (September): 24-38 (Marvin E. Wolfgang, issue editor).

Laqueur, Walter. 1978. "The Futility of Terrorism." In *Contemporary Terrorism: Selected Readings*, edited by John D. Elliot and Leslie K. Gibson, 285-292. Gaithersburg, Maryland: International Association of Chiefs of Police.

Lasswell, Harold D. 1978. "Terrorism and the Political Process." *Terrorism: An International Journal* 1, nos. 3/4: 255-263.

Lebow, Richard Ned. 1983. "The Cuban Missile Crisis: Reading the Lessons Correctly." *Political Science Quarterly* 98, no. 3 (Fall): 431-458.

Leites, Nathan. 1979. "Understanding the Next Act." *Terrorism: An International Journal* 3, nos. 1/2: 1-46.

Levi, Werner. 1976. *Law and Politics in the International Society*. Beverly Hills: Sage.

Livingston, Marius, with Lee Bruce Kress, and Marie G. Wanek, eds. 1978. *International Terrorism in the Contemporary World*. Westport, Connecticut: Greenwood Press.

Livingstone, Neil C. 1982. *The War against Terrorism*. Lexington, Massachusetts: Lexington Books.

Lumbsden, Malvern. 1983. "Sources of Violence in the International System." In *International Violence*, edited by Tunde Adeniran and Yonah Alexander, 3-19. New York: Praeger.

Mallin, Jay. 1978. "Terrorism as a Military Weapon." In *Contemporary Terrorism: Selected Readings*, edited by John D. Elliot and Leslie K. Gibson, 117-128. Gaithersburg, Maryland: International Association of Chiefs of Police.

Mansbach, Richard W., Yale Ferguson, and Donald E. Lampert. 1976. *The Web of World Politics: Nonstate Actors in the Global System*. Englewood Cliffs, New Jersey: Prentice-Hall.

Marighella, Carlos. 1971. *Minimanual of the Urban Guerrilla*. Reprinted as an appendix in *Urban Guerrilla Warfare*, by Robert Moss, 19-42. Adelphi Paper-79. London: The International Institute for Strategic Studies.

McClure, Brooks. 1978. "Terrorism Today and Tomorrow: Prognosis and Treatment." In *Contemporary Terrorism: Selected Readings*, edited by John D. Elliot and Leslie K. Gibson, 293-297. Gaithersburg, Maryland: International Association of Chiefs of Police.

McDonald, Ambassador John W., Jr. 1983. "The United Nations Convention Against the Taking of Hostages: The Inside Story." *Terrorism: An International Journal* 6, no. 4 (Theme issue: United Nations Cooperation against Terrorism; Amos Yoder, guest editor): 545-559.

Merari, Ariel. 1978. "A Classification of Terrorist Groups." *Terrorism: An International Journal* 1, nos. 3/4: 331-346.

Mickolus, Edward F. 1977a. "International Terrorism: Review and Projection." Address to the Conference on Terrorism and the American Corporation, January 11-12, Los Angeles.

Mickolus, Edward F. 1977b. "Reflections on the Study of Terrorism." Paper presented to the Panel on Violence and Terror of the Conference on Complexity: A Challenge to the Adaptive Capacity of American Society, 1776–1976, sponsored by the Society for General Systems Research, March 24-26, Columbia, Maryland.

Mickolus, Edward F. 1977c. "Statistical Approaches to the Study of Terrorism." In *Terrorism: Interdisciplinary Perspectives*, edited by Yonah Alexander and Seymour Maxwell Finger, 209-269. New York: The John Jay Press.

Mickolus, Edward F. 1978a. "Chronology of Transnational Attacks upon American Business People, 1968–1976." *Terrorism: An International Journal* 1, no. 2: 217-235.

Mickolus, Edward F. 1978b. "An Events Data Base for Studying Transnational Terrorism." In *Quantitative Approaches to Political Intelligence: The CIA Experience*, edited by Richards J. Heuer, Jr., 127-163. Boulder, Colorado: Westview Press.

Mickolus, Edward F. 1978c. "Negotiating for Hostages: A Policy Dilemma." In *Contemporary Terrorism: Selected Readings*, edited by John D. Elliot and Leslie K. Gibson, 207-221. Gaithersburg, Maryland: International Association of Chiefs of Police.

Mickolus, Edward F. 1978d. "Trends in Transnational Terrorism." In *International Terrorism in the Contemporary World*, edited by Marius H. Livingston, with Lee Bruce Kress, and Marie G. Wanek, 44-73. Westport, Connecticut: Greenwood Press.

Mickolus, Edward F. 1979a. "Chronology of Transnational Attacks upon American Business People, 1968–1978." In *Political Terrorism and Business: The Threat and Response*, edited by Yonah Alexander and Robert A. Kilmarx, 491-521. New York: Praeger.

Mickolus, Edward F. 1979b. "Transnational Terrorism." In *The Politics of Terrorism*, edited by Michael Stohl, 147-190. New York: Marcel Dekker.

Mickolus, Edward F. 1980. *Transnational Terrorism: A Chronology of Events, 1968–1979*. Westport, Connecticut: Greenwood Press.

Mickolus, Edward F. 1981. "Combatting International Terrorism: A Quantitative Analysis." Ph.D. diss., Yale University.

Mickolus, Edward F. 1982. *International Terrorism: Attributes of Terrorist Events, 1968–1977*. Ann Arbor, Michigan: Inter-University Consortium for Political and Social Research.

Mickolus, Edward F. 1983. "Tracking the Growth and Prevalence of International Terrorism." In *Managing Terrorism: Strategies for the Corporate Executive*, edited by Patrick J. Montana and George S. Roukis, 3-22. Westport, Connecticut: Greenwood Press.

Mickolus, Edward F., and Edward Heyman. 1981. "ITERATE: Monitoring Transnational Terrorism." In *Behavioral and Quantitative Perspectives on Terrorism*, edited by Yonah Alexander and John M. Gleason, 153-174. New York: Pergamon Press.

Mickolus, Edward F., Edward Heyman, and James Schlotter. 1980. "Responding to Terrorism: Basic and Applied Research." In *Responding to the Terrorist Threat: Security and Crisis Management*, edited by Richard H. Shultz and Stephen Sloan, 174-189. New York: Pergamon Press.

Midlarsky, Manus, Martha Crenshaw, and Fumihiko Yoshida. 1980.

"Why Violence Spreads: The Contagion of International Terrorism." *International Studies Quarterly* 24, no. 2 (June): 262-298.

Milbank, David L. 1978. "International and Transnational Terrorism: Diagnosis and Prognosis." In *Contemporary Terrorism: Selected Readings*, edited by John D. Elliot and Leslie K. Gibson, 51-80. Gaithersburg, Maryland: International Association of Chiefs of Police.

Moe, Terry M. 1980. *The Organization of Interests*. Chicago: University of Chicago Press.

Monroe, Charles P. 1982. "Addressing Terrorism in the United States." *Annals of the American Academy of Political and Social Science* 463 (September): 141-148 (Marvin E. Wolfgang, issue editor).

Montana, Patrick J., and George S. Roukis, eds. 1983. *Managing Terrorism: Strategies for the Corporate Executive*. Westport, Connecticut: Greenwood Press.

Netanyahu, Benjamin, ed. 1981. *International Terrorism: Challenge and Response*. New Brunswick, New Jersey: Transaction Books.

Nye, Joseph S., and Robert O. Keohane. 1971a. "Transnational Relations and World Politics: An Introduction." *International Organization* 25, no. 3 (Summer): 329-349 (Joseph S. Nye and Robert O. Keohane, guest editors).

Nye, Joseph S., and Robert O. Keohane. 1971b. "Transnational Relations and World Politics: A Conclusion." *International Organization* 25, no. 3 (Summer): 721-748 (Joseph S. Nye and Robert O. Keohane, guest editors).

O'Ballance, Edgar O. 1978. "Terrorism: The New Growth Form of Warfare." In *International Terrorism in the Contemporary World*, edited by Marius H. Livingston, with Lee Bruce Kress, and Marie G. Wanek, 415-420. Westport, Connecticut: Greenwood Press.

Olson, Mancur, Jr. 1971. *The Logic of Collective Action: Public Goods and the Theory of Groups*. Cambridge: Harvard University Press.

Olson, Mancur, Jr., and Richard Zeckhauser. 1966. "An Economic Theory of Alliances." *Review of Economics and Statistics* 48: 266-279.

Oots, Kent Layne. 1983. "An Exchange Theory of Representation within Interest Groups." *Journal of Political Science* 11, no. 1 (Fall): 15-26.

Oots, Kent Layne, and Thomas C. Wiegele. 1985. "Terrorist and Victim: Psychiatric and Physiological Approaches from a Social

Science Perspective." *Terrorism: An International Journal* 8, no. 1: 1–32.

Osayimwese, Iz. 1983. "An Economic Analysis of International Violence." In *International Violence*, edited by Tunde Adeniran and Yonah Alexander, 182-197. New York: Praeger.

Osmond, Russell Lowell. 1978. "Terrorism and Political Violence Theory: A Quantitative Examination." Paper presented to the Joint National Meeting of the Operations Research Society of America and the Institute of Management Sciences, May 1-3, New York.

Osmond, Russell Lowell. 1979. "Transnational Terrorism 1968–1974: A Quantitative Analysis." Ph.D. diss., Syracuse University.

Passow, Sam. 1984. "Protecting Corporate America from Terrorism." *New York Times*, May 6, 1984, 14F-15F.

Paust, Jordan J. 1977. "A Definitional Focus." In *Terrorism: Interdisciplinary Perspectives*, edited by Yonah Alexander and Seymour Maxwell Finger, 18-29. New York: The John Jay Press.

Pierre, Andrew J. 1976. "The Politics of International Terrorism." *Orbis* 19, no. 4 (Winter): 1251-1269.

Pierre, Andrew J. 1978. "The Politics of International Terrorism." In *Contemporary Terrorism: Selected Readings*, edited by John D. Elliot and Leslie K. Gibson, 35-50. Gaithersburg, Maryland: International Association of Chiefs of Police.

Quainton, The Honorable Anthony C. E. 1983. "Terrorism and Political Violence: A Permanent Challenge to Governments." In *Terrorism, Legitimacy and Power: The Consequences of Political Violence*, edited by Martha Crenshaw, 52-64. Middletown, Connecticut: Wesleyan University Press.

Rapoport, David. 1977. "The Politics of Atrocity." In *Terrorism: Interdisciplinary Perspectives*, edited by Yonah Alexander and Seymour Maxwell Finger, 46-61. New York: The John Jay Press.

Redlick, Amy Sands. 1979. "The Transnational Flow of Information as a Cause of Terrorism." In *Terrorism: Theory and Practice*, edited by Yonah Alexander, David Carlton, and Paul Wilkinson, 73-95. Boulder, Colorado: Westview Press.

Riker, William H. 1962. *The Theory of Political Coalitions*. New Haven, Connecticut: Yale University Press.

Roeder, Philip G. 1982. "Rational Revolution: Extensions of the 'By-Product' Theory of Revolutionary Involvement." *Western Political Quarterly* 35, no. 1 (March): 5-23.

Rosenau, James N., Vincent Davis, and Maurice East, eds. 1972. *The Analysis of International Relations*. New York: Macmillan.

Russell, Charles A. 1983. "Businesses Becoming Increasing Targets."

In *Managing Terrorism: Strategies for the Corporate Executive*, edited by Patrick J. Montana and George S. Roukis, 55-72. Westport, Connecticut: Greenwood Press.

Russell, Charles A., and Bowman H. Miller. 1978. "Profile of a Terrorist." In *Contemporary Terrorism: Selected Readings*, edited by John D. Elliot and Leslie K. Gibson, 81-95. Gaithersburg, Maryland: International Association of Chiefs of Police.

Salert, Barbara. 1976. *Four Theories: Revolutions and Revolutionaries*. New York: Elsevier.

Salisbury, Robert H. 1969. "An Exchange Theory of Interest Groups." *Midwest Journal of Political Science* 13: 1-32.

Sandler, Todd, John T. Tschirhart, and Jon Cauley. 1983. "A Theoretical Analysis of Transnational Terrorism." *American Political Science Review* 77, no. 1 (March): 36-54.

Scalapino, Robert A. 1983. "The Political-Strategic Outlook for International Violence." In *International Violence*, edited by Tunde Adeniran and Yonah Alexander, 165-181. New York: Praeger.

Shamwell, Horace F., Jr. 1983. "Implementation of the Convention on the Prevention and Punishment of Crimes against Internationally Protected Persons, Including Diplomatic Agents." *Terrorism: An International Journal* 6, no. 4 (Theme issue: United Nations Cooperation against Terrorism; Amos Yoder, guest editor): 529-543.

Shribman, David. 1984. "The Textbook Approach to Terrorism." *New York Times*, April 22, 1984, 16E.

Shultz, Richard H., Jr. 1978. "Conceptualizing Political Terrorism: A Typology." *Journal of International Affairs* 32, no. 1 (Spring): 7-15.

Shultz, Richard H., Jr., and Stephen Sloan. 1980a. "International Terrorism: The Nature of the Threat." In *Responding to the Terrorist Threat: Security and Crisis Management*, edited by Richard H. Shultz and Stephen Sloan, 1-17. New York: Pergamon Press.

Shultz, Richard H., Jr., and Stephen Sloan, eds. 1980b. *Responding to the Terrorist Threat: Security and Crisis Management*. New York: Pergamon Press.

Skjelsbaek, Kjell. 1971. "The Growth of International Nongovernmental Organization in the Twentieth Century." *International Organization* 25, no. 3 (Summer): 420-442 (Joseph S. Nye and Robert O. Keohane, guest editors).

Sloan, Stephen. 1978. "International Terrorism: Academic Quest, Operational Art and Policy Implications." *Journal of International Affairs* 32, no. 1 (Spring): 1-5.

Sloan, Stephen. 1980. "Simulating Terrorism: An Analysis of Findings Related to Tactical, Behavioral, and Administrative Responses of Participating Police and Military Forces." In *Responding to the Terrorist Threat: Security and Crisis Management*, edited by Richard H. Shultz and Stephen Sloan, 115-133. New York: Pergamon Press.

Sloan, Stephen. 1981. *Simulating Terrorism*. Norman: University of Oklahoma Press.

Sloan, Stephen, Richard Kearney, and Charles Wise. 1978. "Learning about Terrorism: Simulations and Future Directions." *Terrorism: An International Journal* 1, nos. 3/4: 315-329.

Smart, I. M. H. 1978. "The Power of Terror." In *Contemporary Terrorism: Selected Readings*, edited by John D. Elliot and Leslie K. Gibson, 25-33. Gaithersburg, Maryland: International Association of Chiefs of Police.

Snitch, Thomas H. 1982. "Terrorism and Political Assassinations: A Transnational Assessment, 1968–80." *Annals of the American Academy of Political and Social Science* 463 (September): 54-68 (Marvin E. Wolfgang, issue editor).

Sterling, Claire. 1981. *The Terror Network*. New York: Holt, Rinehart, and Winston.

Stiles, Dennis W. 1978. "Sovereignty and the New Violence." In *Contemporary Terrorism: Selected Readings*, edited by John D. Elliot and Leslie K. Gibson, 261-267. Gaithersburg, Maryland: International Association of Chiefs of Police.

Stohl, Michael. 1979a. "Introduction: Myths and Realities of Political Terrorism." In *The Politics of Terrorism*, edited by Michael Stohl, 1-19. New York: Marcel Dekker.

Stohl, Michael, ed. 1979b. *The Politics of Terrorism*. New York: Marcel Dekker.

Stokey, Edith B., and Richard Zeckhauser. 1978. *A Primer for Policy Analysis*. New York: W. W. Norton and Company.

Targ, Harry. 1979. "Social Structure and Revolutionary Terrorism: A Preliminary Investigation." In *The Politics of Terrorism*, edited by Michael Stohl, 119-143. New York: Marcel Dekker.

Taylor, Stuart, Jr. 1984. "Reagan Sends Congress Four Bills Aimed at International Terrorism." *New York Times*, April 27, 1984, 1 *et passim*.

Thompson, W. Scott. 1976. "Political Violence and the Correlation of Forces." *Orbis* 19, no. 4 (Winter): 1270-1288.

Tullock, Gordon. 1971. "The Paradox of Revolution." *Public Choice* 11: 89-99.

Tullock, Gordon. 1972. *Toward a Mathematics of Politics*. Ann Arbor: University of Michigan Press.

Turk, Austin T. 1982. "Social Dynamics of Terrorism." *Annals of the*

American Academy of Political and Social Science 463 (September): 119-128 (Marvin E. Wolfgang, issue editor).

Wardlaw, Grant. 1982. *Political Terrorism: Theory, Tactics and Counter-Measures*. New York: Cambridge University Press.

Watson, Francis M. 1976. *Political Terrorism: The Threat and Response*. Washington: Robert B. Luce Company.

Wilkinson, Paul. 1979a. "Social Scientific Theory and Civil Violence." In *Terrorism: Theory and Practice*, edited by Yonah Alexander, David Carlton, and Paul Wilkinson, 45-72. Boulder, Colorado: Westview Press.

Wilkinson, Paul. 1979b. "Terrorist Movements." In *Terrorism: Theory and Practice*, edited by Yonah Alexander, David Carlton, and Paul Wilkinson, 99-117. Boulder, Colorado: Westview Press.

Winn, Gregory F. T. 1981. "Terrorism, Alienation and German Society." In *Behavioral and Quantitative Perspectives on Terrorism*, edited by Yonah Alexander and John M. Gleason, 256-282. New York: Pergamon Press.

Wolf, John B. 1978a. "Organization and Management Practices of Urban Terrorist Groups." *Terrorism: An International Journal* 1, no. 2: 169-186.

Wolf, John B. 1978b. "Terrorist Manipulation of the Democratic Process." In *International Terrorism in the Contemporary World*, edited by Marius H. Livingston, with Lee Bruce Kress, and Marie G. Wanek, 297-306. Westport, Connecticut: Greenwood Press.

Wolfers, Arnold. 1959. "The Actors in International Politics." In *Theoretical Aspects of International Relations*, edited by William T. R. Fox, 83-106. Notre Dame, Indiana: University of Notre Dame Press.

Wright, Steve. 1981. "A Multivariate Time Series Analysis of the Northern Ireland Conflict 1969–1976." In *Behavioral and Quantitative Perspectives on Terrorism*, edited by Yonah Alexander and John M. Gleason, 283-328. New York: Pergamon Press.

Yoder, Amos. 1983a. "The Effectiveness of U.N. Action against International Terrorism: Conclusions and Comments." *Terrorism: An International Journal* 6, no. 4 (Theme issue: United Nations Cooperation against Terrorism; Amos Yoder, guest editor): 587-592.

Yoder, Amos. 1983b. "United Nations Resolutions against International Terrorism." *Terrorism: An International Journal* 6, no. 4 (Theme issue: United Nations Cooperation against Terrorism; Amos Yoder, guest editor): 503-517.

Young, Oran R. 1972. "The Actors in World Politics." In *The Analysis of International Politics*, edited by James N. Rosenau, Vincent Davis, and Maurice East, 125-144. New York: Macmillan.
Zawodny, J. K. 1978. "Internal Organization Problems and the Sources of Tension in Terrorist Movements as Catalysts for Violence." *Terrorism: An International Journal* 1, nos. 3/4: 275-285.

INDEX

About the Author

KENT LAYNE OOTS, Visiting Assistant Professor of Political Science, Texas A&M University, is co-author of *Leaders Under Stress: A Psychophysiological Examination of International Crises* and the author or co-author of articles in the *Journal of Political Science* and *Terrorism*.